# ADVENTUROUS PUB WALKS
## IN
# ESSEX

**Ann and Norman Skinner**

COUNTRYSIDE BOOKS
NEWBURY BERKSHIRE

First published 2003
© Ann and Norman Skinner 2003

COUNTRYSIDE BOOKS
3 Catherine Road
Newbury, Berkshire

To view our complete range of books,
please visit us at
www.countrysidebooks.co.uk

ISBN 1 85306 785 7

Designed by Peter Davies, Nautilus Design
Maps and photographs by Ann Skinner

Typeset by Techniset Typesetters, Newton-le-Willows
Produced through MRM Associates Ltd., Reading
Printed by Woolnough Bookbinding Ltd., Irthlingborough

# Contents

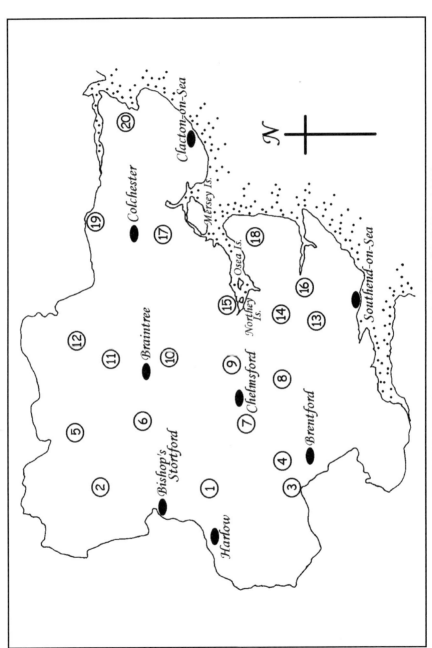

**AREA MAP SHOWING THE LOCATION OF THE WALKS**

**PUBLISHER'S NOTE**

We hope that you obtain considerable enjoyment from this book; great care has been taken in its preparation. Although at the time of publication all routes followed public rights of way or permitted paths, diversion orders can be made and permissions withdrawn.

We cannot, of course, be held responsible for such diversion orders and any inaccuracies in the text which result from these or any other changes to the routes nor any damage which might result from walkers trespassing on private property. We are anxious though that all details covering the walks are kept up to date and would therefore welcome information from readers which would be relevant to future editions.

The simple sketch maps that accompany the walks in this book are based on notes made by the authors whilst checking out the routes on the ground. However, for the benefit of a proper map, we do recommend that you purchase the relevant Ordnance Survey sheet covering your walk. The Ordnance Survey maps are widely available, especially through booksellers and local newsagents.

# Introduction

What a time we have had planning, exploring, and preparing this, our latest book. Of all the books we have been involved with, this has been the most exciting and most exhilarating. We spoke at length with rambling friends eager to know what we were up to that was taking so much of our time and energy. We got various pieces of sage advice to spice things up and make it more adventurous like 'give them the wrong map', 'finish the walk's description halfway round', 'tell them the wrong starting point'. We hasten to add that all these suggestions we immediately ignored! What we did do was to draw up a list of places we would like to visit. We then started our paper research – routes were designed and plans made. The adventure had begun and the result is 20 walks that take you over some of the best countryside that Essex has to offer.

All the walks in the book are between 8 and 12 miles in length and the route directions have been broken down into numbered sections. You will find each of these numbers on the accompanying sketch map to indicate where each section starts and, at the end of each section, we have indicated the distance covered so you can pace yourself. The sketch maps give you an overview of the route to be followed but we recommend that you also arm yourself with the relevant Ordnance Survey map. This will give you the benefit of more detailed information and is especially useful for identifying the main features of views. You will find that we often use the word 'twitten', which we think is a lovely word. It describes a fenced or hedged path that runs through a housing estate.

Since these routes are that bit longer, we feel that everyone would welcome the chance to rest and recharge their batteries. Therefore, a pub stop is suggested roughly halfway round the circuit. The featured pubs vary tremendously in size, style and the facilities they offer. However, we have visited them all and can heartily recommend them for their warm welcome and good food. Telephone numbers are given so you can check opening times and menus. Some do get busy at weekends, so it may be advisable to book ahead.

Before you set off on your adventure, remember that the countryside and the weather are constantly changing so go prepared. Have you chosen the most appropriate footwear: walking shoes, boots or even wellingtons? In spring and autumn you will undoubtedly encounter some muddy patches. In late August the farmer may have just ploughed the ground and you may encounter a bumpy path during his 14 day reinstatement period. A good pair of walking boots will stand you in good stead on such an occasion. Maybe you will be walking in balmy June wearing your best new shorts only to be surrounded by a host of eager stinging nettles. You know what we mean! So dress accordingly. Do you have emergency rainwear? You can get a lightweight pack these days that just slips in a pocket and may well save you a drenching. Have you a sun hat for those lovely sunny days or an umbrella for when heavy rain may make map reading hard? And, don't forget that in winter the temperature can suddenly drop even lower, so gloves and one of the famous walker's hats may make life seem a bit more rosy.

Do you have a drink in case you get thirsty? If you are planning a picnic remember to put food in a firm container so it arrives in an edible condition. Tighten the tops of drinks containers; it is most annoying to get a wet back and nothing to drink! We have all been *there*! In addition, we would recommend you carry a compass and a couple of carrier bags. You can cover your muddy boots with them at lunchtime or have them as a seat for mid-morning or afternoon break. In the autumn you may well want to use them as a harvest basket for sloes, blackberries, etc. The other item we always like to have with us is our trusty camera. What adventures we have shared over the years.

Like the TV programmes which show the takes that did not work, we occasionally discovered routes which, for one reason or another, had to be discarded in favour of what we view as improvements. As a result we think that we have possibly covered all the best available paths and all the best available pubs in these routes throughout Essex. At any rate we do recommend you to tackle these slightly longer walks. A great sense of achievement will accompany the completion of a walk in this book.

Happy walking!

Ann and Norman Skinner

# MATCHING GREEN TO HATFIELD HEATH

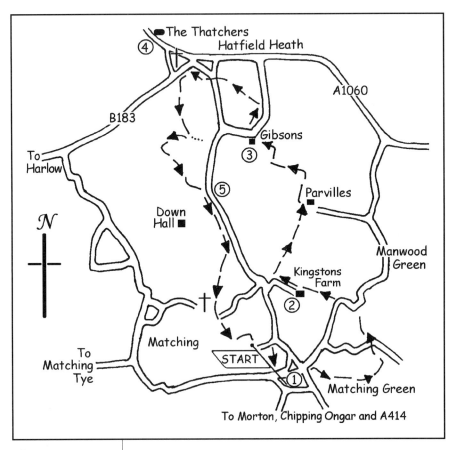

**Distance:**
8¹/₄ miles

**Starting point:**
In the north-west
corner of the green
in Matching Green.
GR 535111

**Map: OS Explorer 183 Chelmsford & The Rodings**

**How to get there:** *From Harlow, take the B183 towards
Hatfield Heath. Turn off at Sheering and go through
Matching Tye to arrive at Matching Green. From the A414 at
Chipping Ongar, turn off the B184 at Shelley and continue
through Moreton, following signs for Matching Green.*

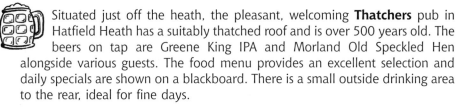

Situated just off the heath, the pleasant, welcoming **Thatchers** pub in Hatfield Heath has a suitably thatched roof and is over 500 years old. The beers on tap are Greene King IPA and Morland Old Speckled Hen alongside various guests. The food menu provides an excellent selection and daily specials are shown on a blackboard. There is a small outside drinking area to the rear, ideal for fine days.

**Telephone:** *01279 730270.*

 *The Walk*

① Make your way east across the green towards a large pond. Take the road signposted to **Matching Airfield**, soon reaching the gates of **Stock Hall** on the right. Go through the open gates and immediately turn right at a waymark towards a fence. Through the fence turn left and walk with the fence on your left. When the fence turns to the left continue across the field to a red-brick airfield building. Pass by the building and bear right to two large gateposts. Now turn left up the farm track to a road.

The Matchings consist of three delightful villages to the south of Hatfield Heath – Matching, Matching Green and Matching Tye, all part of a lovely and lonely countryside. Matching, visited towards the end of the walk, is one of the gems of the county, with two greens, a medieval cottage, an attractive gabled house, a 17th-century barn across a moat, and a church hidden away within field gates. Opposite the church stands Matching Hall, its moat dug by Saxon settlers so that the deep ditch could serve as a defence against Viking raiders. Our route starts from the very large green in Matching Green, passing Stock Hall to the east and out onto the wartime airfield. We head north to Peartree Green and then west to join part of the Forest Way, continuing past a fine old house, Parvilles. Then it is on to the village of Hatfield Heath for lunch, after which we head south across the heath to visit Matching's lovely church and the famous medieval Marriage Feast Room. This is a really fine walk which gives plenty of opportunities to treasure the beauty, the sights and the buildings in the Essex countryside.

THE CHURCH AT MATCHING IS WELL WORTH VISITING

*Matching Airfield was one of hundreds of airfields built throughout East Anglia in the Second World War. Many of these were for bombers and so, as the offensive progressed quickly into France and Germany, the bases were relocated to France and the English sites closed down. In the case of personnel from the USA this meant a short stay in England and many a broken heart for the English girls. There are still artefacts and other memorabilia around to remind us of those historic days.*

Turn left along the road for 130

yards. To the right you can see **White Roding church and windmill**. At a waymark turn right over a field to the far hedge. Here a hedged bridleway runs to the right. Often this can be quite muddy so we suggest you walk north with the hedge on your left to the road. Turn left for 100 yards. At a left-hand bend turn right on a public byway. This 500 yard route to **Kingstons Farm** can be quite hard going, especially in the winter months but it is worth persevering! (2 miles)

② Walk through the farm buildings (now commercial units) and continue on a metalled track for 150 yards. At a footpath sign turn right along the **Forest Way**. Follow this pleasant green lane for some time to the delightful **Parvilles Farm**. Turn left, then right past the main building on your left. Soon, fine views over the landscape can be enjoyed. Walk downhill with the hedge on your right. The path follows the hedge, turning left and left again to a bridge. In recent years a large reservoir has been constructed and clearly local people walk parallel to the footpath on the banks. Cross the bridge and turn right and left on a good field edge path to **Gibsons Farm**. (1½ miles)

③ Continue to the right up a lane. Opposite **Friars Farm** turn left along the footpath. The route follows the edge of the field, turning right at the end and round a thicket. At a waymark, turn left through the hedge and follow the path across a small grassy field to a metal gate. Do not turn right here but go left past a gate and continue west along a broad track to a road. Cross the road onto the heath at **Hatfield Heath** and make for the church 500 yards ahead. Cross another road and go past the church over yet another road. The **Thatchers** pub is a few yards along Stortford Road. (1¼ miles)

*The wide-spreading village green in Hatfield Heath makes an ideal cricket pitch, at least from the spectators' point of view. There are not many areas described as heaths in Essex. This one is a splendidly open spot for passers-by to enjoy.*

④ After your lunch break, cross over the heath and follow **Pond Lane** southwards. Opposite the end of this lane, beside the large mansion, Peggerells, is a new bungalow. At its gates two footpaths are waymarked. The right-hand one passes over the gravel path in front of the bungalow to a narrow gate on the right-hand side of the garage. Go through this gate and follow the path to the side of the garden fence. Go through a second gate and, at a fence, cross a ditch to walk downhill with a deep ditch on the left to a waymark by a stream. Turn left with this stream on your right and soon come to another waymark. Turn right

THE THATCHERS, HATFIELD HEATH

carefully down steps cut in the bank and cross a plank bridge to follow a waymark pointing uphill. Continue for 300 yards. Turn left with the **Stort Valley Way** sign and follow this downhill towards the large **Downhall Wood**. At **Pincey Brook** turn left and follow the path on the edge of the brook to **Downhall Road**. (1$^1/_2$ miles)

⑤ Turn right and walk up a hill, passing the entrance to **Parvilles**. Further on downhill turn right along a footpath to a stile. Cross an earth bridge by a deep ditch and turn left along the line of this between two woods. A waymark through a hedge on the right leads to a field edge path. Nearer **Matching church** turn left over a bridge and into the churchyard. The path goes straight through the churchyard to another footpath opposite.

*It is worth a detour to the right at this point to visit the church and the Marriage Feast Room. The church was founded by the Dean of St Paul's over 700 years ago and its tower was added in the 15th century. The Feast Room can be found in the long building you can see between the church and the green. In medieval times, a Matching man by the name of William Chimney decided to make the weddings of this village very pleasant events indeed. He built a large room above four smaller rooms, and to this upper room the brides and grooms of the village have climbed for 500 years to feast with their friends. It has an open king post roof and is a notable survival from the Middle Ages.*

Cross the stile opposite the church and walk past **Matching Hall**. Cross another stile and join the left-hand end of the facing thicket. Turn left and walk to the waymark. At this point turn right towards **Brick House**. Now turn left down a farm lane past a crossing hedge. Turn right at a waymark and walk by a field edge towards a playing field. Over the playing field turn left to find a path on the right between a garden and a wood. This leads to a road and you will see the large green at **Matching Green**. Here make your way back to your car. (2 miles)

*Date walk completed:*

# WIDDINGTON TO WICKEN BONHUNT

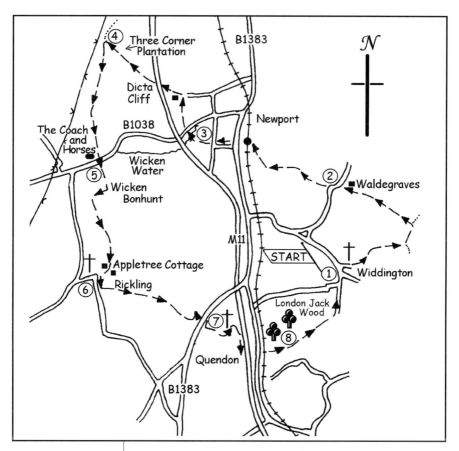

**Distance:**
11¼ miles

**Starting point:**
*High Street,*
*Widdington.*
*GR 539317*

**Map: OS Explorer 195 Braintree & Saffron Walden**

**How to get there:** *Widdington lies 2 miles east of the B1383 to the south of Newport. Look for the brown visitor signs for the Mole Hall Wildlife Centre and follow the road round to Widdington's High Street. You should be able to park in the road, but be careful not to block any driveways.*

QUENDON PARISH CHURCH

*T*his delightful walk begins in the quiet village of Widdington and follows footpaths over wide fields to pick up a high level byway, followed by a pretty descent into Newport. You are only in town for the briefest of visits before you make your way west and under the M11 on a good path out into the middle of nowhere or so it seems. Another bridleway takes you south and down into Wicken Bonhunt where a warm welcome awaits you at the Coach and Horses inn. After lunch another long, straight path proceeds south again, offering good open views to Rickling with its ancient church. You join the Harcamlow Way to the outskirts of Quendon and then walk through this charming village and pass another lovely church. A few nifty lefts and rights bring you back under the M11 and up a long gravelled horse ride into Widdington.

The delightfully thatched **Coach and Horses** at Wicken Bonhunt stands high from the road in the centre of the village. There are several small bars inside the pub and a pleasant eating area outside. An interesting blackboard menu offers a good choice of main meals and snacks, and a well-kept range of beers is also available.

**Telephone:** *01799 540516.*

*Widdington has a pretty collection of old buildings, among them 15th-century Widdington Hall, now a farm with a Tudor barn, and Prior's Hall, a farmhouse whose stone walls behind plaster are believed to be as old as Magna Carta. Prior's Hall Barn (English Heritage) is open to the public at weekends in the summer months. Mole Hall, a moated house lying about 1 mile south-east of the village, is said to be a perfect example of the Elizabethan hall in Essex. Its grounds are now well known as a wildlife park, open throughout the year (telephone: 01799 540400).*

① Walking north up the **High Street**, turn right into **Church Lane** and pass **Widdington church**.

*Widdington church has a Norman window opening to a 15th-century vestry. The church was restored and the tower rebuilt with bold gargoyles and handsome pinnacles. Behind the altar is a 14th-century window with fine carving round it. Another window, of 14th-century glass, has shields of France and England. There is a 750 year old piscina*

Turn left at the footpath post at the end of the churchyard wall and then right to walk with a ditch on your right. At the yellow arrow turn left to walk under the power lines and then right at the next yellow arrow. At the end of the ditch go straight on and cross an open field diagonally half left to the hedge and yellow arrow. Turn right on a gently descending path to a junction of paths. Turn left with a ditch on your left – a yellow arrow confirms your route is straight on – to pass a pretty thatched cottage. Immediately turn left down a byway, which can be muddy at times. Your right of way, the byway, goes right on the right of a hedge, and then shortly left again to regain the original track. Pass an old barn and cottage and keep straight on – ignore paths off to the right and left – and in about 1/2 mile pass **Waldegraves Farm** and walk out onto the road. (2 miles)

② Continue in a westerly direction off the road again by a concrete direction post and along another westerly downhill path for about a mile. Enjoy the gentle downhill path, with super views all the way into **Newport**. Leave the open fields to enter a sort of footpath tunnel at the side of a field as you descend to the quarry. Turn right into **Quarry Road**, which can be busy with lorries during working hours; so take care. Just past **Briars Cottage** come to a white wicket fence and turn left; go up the steps and over the railway bridge. You are now at **Newport station**.

*Newport lies on the original coaching route from London to Cambridge and as such is littered with old inns. The town stands on the River Cam, which rises near Widdington. Its interesting buildings include Monks Barn, a private house built in red brick with dark beams overhanging the pavements. It is noted for the carving in the wooden arch of its studded door. The church dates from the 13th century and a detour to see it would be well worthwhile. It contains a 550 year old screen and a 450 year old Flemish carving of the Crucifixion.*

*Among the other treasures is a tablet for Joseph Smith of nearby Shortgrove Hall, who was private secretary to Pitt.*

From the station walk west along **Station Road**, cross over the B1383 near the Esso garage and walk ahead up **Frambury Lane** onto a housing estate. Turn right at the T-junction and after a high privet hedge at number 61 turn left. At the footpath sign, walk into the field to keep the hedge on your right. When you come to a yellow arrow turn right and walk out to the B1038. (1 3/4 miles)

③ Cross the road and head half left to the ford over **Wicken Water**. You will be pleased to hear there is a sturdy footbridge here. Your onward route is half right over the cross-field path and along a track. As you pass **Dicta Cliff** look out for the footpath sign. Turn left towards the M11; here the track can be muddy at times. This takes you under the motorway and on a steady climb north-west for about 1/2 mile, passing a strange triangular wood called **Three Corner Plantation**. (1 1/4 miles)

④ At the bottom of the dip, well before the power lines, there is a footpath junction where a sharp turn left, south, takes you almost back on yourself. This long track of about a mile brings you to **Wicken Bonhunt** and lunch. Turn right for a few yards when you reach the road to find the pub. (1½ miles)

⑤ Well fed and rested cross the road and take the path opposite the pub over the stream and up the hill on a track. When you come to the bridleway sign, turn right with a hedge on your right. At the next corner go left and right to follow the track south all the way to the road and bridleway sign. You have now reached **Rickling**. Turn right passing **Appletree Cottage** and walk on past the farm to the junction. Your onward route is left but you may wish to go right for a few paces and explore **Rickling**

**church**. It would also make a good place for a picnic. (1¼ miles)

*In the 19th century, a famous murder took place in Rickling. It was in 1898 that Samuel Dougal met relatively wealthy Miss Camille Holland. Somehow he persuaded her to leave London and live with him at Moat Farm. Things went well till she got fed up with him paying attention to so many of the village girls and getting them pregnant. When she complained he took her out for a pony ride and shot her through the head. He buried her in a nearby ditch and continued to live off her money, forging her*

**THE COACH AND HORSES, WICKEN BONHUNT**

*signature. Eventually he was caught, tried at Chelmsford Court and found guilty, ending up on the gallows.*

⑥ Continue south-east till you come to a footpath sign. Turn left and walk with the hedge on your left. At the field corner go straight on over an earth bridge. Do not go right here. You will now find yourself on a well-walked cross-field path. At the end of the field come to a blue arrow and go straight ahead into a dip called **Hanginghill**. Cross a stream and follow the yellow arrow uphill. Ignore the track as it climbs half right; your route is half left uphill on a grassy path. When you come to a house, go left and right round it on a well-signed path, to come out onto the B1383 by a post box and bus stop. You have now arrived at **Quendon**. (1¼ miles)

*Quendon has a 100 acre park where deer have roamed for centuries. The Tudor hall is faced with red and blue bricks and in the grounds are 17th-century painted figures. The church dates from the 13th century. It is of special interest because from 1621 to 1792 they had burials in wool here, as recorded in the register. That of Thomas Winstanley, the father of Henry, who built the Eddystone Lighthouse, was one of them.*

⑦ Walk down Quendon main road till you come to a row of delightful flint and brick cottages. Cross the road with care and take the track ahead, marked '**Quendon Parish Church**'. You will find yourself on a steep uphill climb to the church. Here there is a junction of five paths. Take the one straight ahead with a bridleway sign and a yellow arrow, south-east to a post with a blue arrow. As you enter the next field leave the bridleway which goes straight ahead and turn left with woods on your left for 10 yards until you come to a yellow arrow showing you should turn right on a cross-field path to the wood opposite. You are joining another bridleway and should turn left with trees on your right. At the end of the wood turn left, walk with the hedge on your left for 100 yards to a blue arrow, turn right (east) by the blue arrow for 300 yards, then right again into the middle of a large field for 75 yards. You are very near the M11 now. Turn left towards it at the next blue arrow and leave the lovely track. Your route is slightly downhill, then right, to walk alongside and well below the level of the M11 and out to a lane. Turn left on the lane and pass under the M11. At **North Hall Road** turn left. Just past the entrance to **Home Farm** look on your right for some wooden steps up from the road, pass through some buildings by the home-made footpath sign. Now cross a stile and go up the steps, cross the railway line, go down the steps and over another stile. The footpath goes left then right and you make your way uphill on a path to the left of a huge field with a wood on your left. (1½ miles)

⑧ At the end of **London Jack Wood** you come to a house and Country Landowners sign; go left and immediately right round the house. Your route back to your car is half right up the drive on a gentle rise north-east for more than ½ mile to a bridleway sign. Now head half left under the chestnut trees and down the road. At the junction go straight ahead into **Widdington High Street** to return to your car. (³⁄₄ miles)

*Date walk completed:*

# NAVESTOCK SIDE TO WEALD PARK

**THE KISSING GATE AT THE EXIT FROM THE MORES**

**Distance:**
9 miles

**Starting point:**
*The common at Navestock Side. GR 563973*

Map: OS Explorer 175 Southend-on-Sea & Basildon

**How to get there:** *Navestock Side lies west of the A128 Ongar–Brentwood road, just north of Brentwood. About 3¹/₂ miles north of Wilson's Corner in Brentwood, make a west turn, signed to Navestock Side. After ¹/₄ mile, turn left and pass the Green Man pub. Turn left again at the far end of the common into a narrow back road. Parking can be found along here but please ensure you don't block the access to the cricket pavilion.*

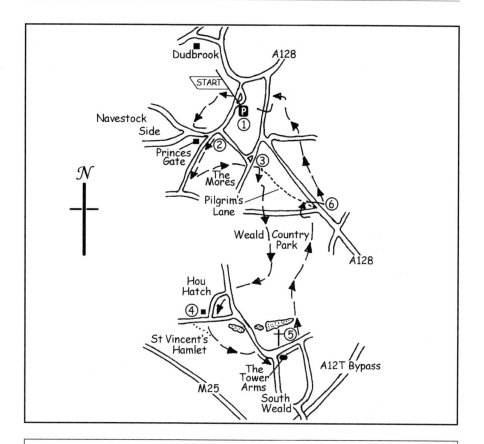

*T*he walk starts at Navestock Side, near the cricket pitch. It's so relaxing on a warm summer's afternoon to just sit and watch a cricket match, don't you think? A treat perhaps for when you return? But this is a glorious walk at any time of year. The route starts by taking you out of the village, along a country road to a shady wood, and then into Weald Country Park. The views across the lake to the impressive building of South Weald church are so enchanting that you could be in Derbyshire or the Lake District. Continuing through wide fields you arrive in South Weald which makes an ideal lunch stop. The final leg of the walk takes you past an 18th-century folly, along a popular byway, across a golf course and finally back to the common in Navestock Side.

The **Tower Arms** at South Weald is a busy family pub. It has a quaint front bar with wooden panelling and there are two further rooms and a conservatory used for meals. You will find a quick and efficient food service here. On offer is a selection of sandwiches and jacket potatoes. For those in search of something more substantial, there is a wide range of meals, including scampi, sausage and steak dishes. What about a drink, you cry! Behind the bar there is Greene King IPA, Young's Special, Strongbow cider and a range of wines by the glass.

**Telephone:** *01277 210266.*

 *The Walk*

① Go over the common and cross the road you drove in on to make your way to the slip road. Turn right and walk in front of the houses on the slip road. Pass the **Green Man** pub to reach a footpath sign. Turn left down the track to the right of the pub where you can enjoy good views over to **Dudbrook**. Those in the know may also make out the tower of the 'secret' nuclear bunker at **Kelvedon Hatch** on your far right.

*Now open to the public, this bunker was built at the start of the Cold War, and would have served as the region's H.Q. in the event of a nuclear attack.*

At the next direction post turn left. You are heading slightly downhill towards another direction post near a gap in the hedge, just right of some tall willow trees. At the yellow arrow go though the gap and slightly left, almost behind the willow trees. You now have to cross a large field which may be in crop but the path should be clear. Head half right (south-west) and out to the road. (³/₄ mile)

② Turn left, pass **Princes Gate** and turn right into **Wheelers Lane**. Continue on the road for about ¹/₂ mile to **The Mores** wood. As the road bends look for a footpath sign on your left.

*When the Woodland Trust put out an appeal we all gave what we could to buy The Mores for public use. It was indeed a well worthwhile venture. You will today take a woodland path to the right of the wood but you may wish to return at a later date to explore the circular route. There is an information board, a few feet after you go through the entrance gate, that tells you about the wildlife you may expect to encounter on your visit.*

Keep to the right of the wood. About halfway down, a public footpath comes across from your left and yellow arrows now mark your route, which is straight on. Cross the bridge. Two more arrows direct you towards the exit, passing the rear of some farm buildings on your right. (1¼ miles)

③ Cross the road into a bridleway marked **'Pilgrim's Lane'**, passing King Bros. Immediately look for a footpath sign and stile on your right. Climb this and walk ahead with a fence on your right. Go over two more stiles to arrive at a large meadow. Cross this diagonally right to a gap in the hedge with a stile on the right. Pass to the right of a pond, where the ground may be muddy. A series of yellow arrows and a fence on your left will bring you to a kissing gate and the road beside house number 113. Cross the main road and make your way into **Weald Country Park** by the back entrance (there is a sign '22–24 Park Lane'). Walk past these cottages and go over a stile. Ignore the footpath sign on your left for footpath 109 and continue ahead to a crossing track. Go straight on to the right of some fir trees. Ignore the bridleway on the right and keep straight on to a junction of paths, with some small yellow arrows marked on posts, and

your first glimpse of the lake. You must turn right here and walk towards the park bench. If you are looking to have a picnic somewhere along your route, this next section is a delightful area for a longer stop. You will find a number of seats put there especially with you in mind. There are magnificent views for the next ½ mile. The track becomes a dry gravel road and, as it bends left, keep right and walk to the right of the keeper's cottage to the road and footpath sign. Cross this road with care as it can be busy at times, and follow the byway, passing **Hou Hatch** on an ancient road. When you come to the main road, turn right into **St Vincent's Hamlet**, passing a bustling working dairy farm. (2 miles)

④ Turn left at the concrete footpath sign, crossing the stile and making your way along the narrow path up the side of a cottage garden to another stile. You are now heading towards a quaint metal stile over the wire fence straight ahead. Go just to the right of the rear of a barn, then go half left, where you will find a wooden bridge over a stream. Walk ahead, crossing the track, then going slightly left and leaving the track **before** the farm gate. Head uphill on an unmarked cross-field path to the stile that is just visible to the left of a distant wood. Go over the stile and make your way across this large field to the left-hand corner of the wood and a further stile. Walk with the fence on your right, following the yellow arrows. Go over a stile, round a pond, straight on through the woods, and over a final stile to the road. Turn right and walk uphill on the narrow 'courtesy path' to the right of the road. You will find the **Tower Arms** public house opposite **South Weald church** near the road junction on your right. (1 mile)

*South Weald church is an impressive building that dominates the skyline. Parts date back to about 1150. A window in the tower has medieval glass, with two panels showing the Sacrifice of Abraham and the Queen of Sheba. Occasionally the tower has been open to the public and we can remember a warm summer afternoon a few years ago when we were lucky enough to pay a visit to the parapet. The views were magnificent.*

⑤ Leave the pub and cross the road. If you have time, you may want to explore the church before finding the high level path just to the left of the busy road. This path brings you to a footpath sign and an entrance to **Weald Country Park**. Turn left. This again is a good place for a picnic. Toilets are

THE TOWER ARMS, SOUTH WEALD

available and it is possible to take a detour to look at an interesting folly. Just before the toilet block turn left and climb up the rather steep hill to the **Belvedere Temple**.

*Belvedere Temple was built on top of the mound in the 1740s. In 1752 the Tower family of the nearby hall built the upstairs to the folly. Writing in 1949, Arthur Mee describes the Tower family home as having been refashioned but still having two 16th-century wings, one with gables and solid looking turrets and one with a parapet and fine chimney. The building unfortunately had to be destroyed in 1950 because it was unsafe. The old deer park, the gardens and the lake have now become the Weald Country Park and it is, of course, fully open to the public. More information about these buildings and the park can be found at the Weald Park Visitor Centre, the entrance to which is opposite where you came out on the road just before lunch.*

Once you have discovered as much as you wish about the history, retrace your steps to the toilets and continue on your walk. Go through the gap in the hedge and make your way northwards. Follow the fence to the edge of the wood and go over a stile. Walk with the wood on your left to an earth bridge over the stream and go through a kissing gate. Follow the yellow arrow uphill on a very wide path. Six trees short of the end of the avenue, turn right under a chestnut tree with a white spot. Walk along this path for just over 100 yards to a crossing track. Go straight ahead, passing a post with a white and red marker (15/AA) and start a gentle descent, keeping right at the first fork.

Follow the route indicated by the yellow arrow, then take a left turn. All the while, you are gently climbing, passing three areas of fir trees on your right. Continue on the main path, ignoring two right turns and one left. When you come to the wooden squeeze gate, keep straight ahead over a crossing horse-ride, then pass a red dog litter box on your left. After 25 yards, look for a yellow arrow hidden on your right and turn right, again keeping to the main path well to the right of some green houses. A bridleway sign brings you out to the road beside a Civic Amenity Site. Turn left and walk carefully up to the crossing road and go over into **Bellhouse Lane**. When this becomes a track, fork right. You have rejoined **Pilgrim's Lane** which is a gravel track. Follow this right to the busy **Ongar Road**. Turn right, cross with care, and then immediately turn left into **Hullett's Lane**. (2 miles)

⑥ Go through two half gates, only passable on foot. Pass lovely **Gents**

**Farm**, built in 1530. The lane is straight ahead for about a mile, north-west then north. It can be muddy at times. You should ignore two footpaths and one bridleway off to your right. When you come to the road, go straight across. Your onward route is marked with a bridleway sign and a yellow arrow. Go up the road, passing **Bentley Cottage** gate. Turn right at a further yellow waymark. You are now entering the golf course. Follow the yellow arrows carefully half left, then slightly left, by two yellow posts at a stream going under some trees. At the next yellow arrow, go half left onto a path between two fairways, heavily wooded on both sides. At the next arrow, turn half right across a fairway to a four-way junction of paths. Turn left to go past the clubhouse and out to the footpath sign by the main road. Cross the busy road near **Kumra Lodge** with care and turn left. After 300 yards, turn right up **Old Crown Lane** and keep ahead as it becomes a track, which can be muddy at times. At the crossing track, turn left on an old road that leads you the easy way back to **Navestock Side**, the cricket pitch and your car. (2 miles)

*Date walk completed:*

# DODDINGHURST TO BLACKMORE

STONDON MASSEY POND OPPOSITE THE BRICKLAYERS ARMS PUB

**Distance:**
8³/₄ miles

**Starting point:**
The village hall car park in Doddinghurst. GR 589990

Maps: OS Explorer 175 Southend-on-Sea & Basildon and 183 Chelmsford & The Rodings

**How to get there:** Doddinghurst lies between Brentwood and Ongar. Take the A128 to Kelvedon Hatch. At the Fox Hatch junction, turn north-east and then follow the local signs into Doddinghurst village centre, heading for the church. The village hall car park is opposite the church.

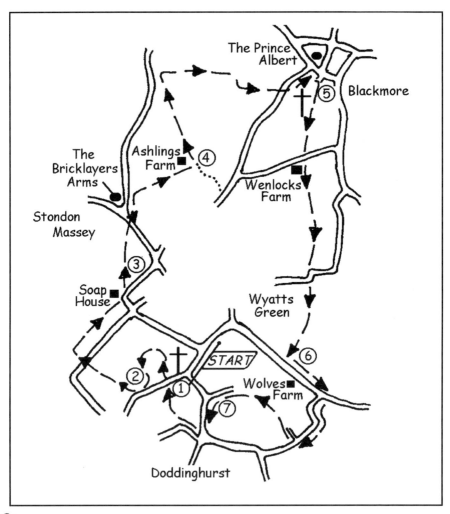

The **Prince Albert** is one of three pubs that can be found in Blackmore village but it is the first one you come to, and you will find most rambler's needs can be met here. There is a wide range of home-cooked food that includes specials, chicken, fish, jacket potatoes and burger dishes. The drinks include Strongbow cider, Carling and Stella Artois lager, Greene King IPA, John Smith's Smooth and Guinness on hand pump.

**Telephone:** *01277 821705.*

This walk visits some very interesting wooded areas starting with Church Wood in Doddinghurst. You will walk along an ancient RUPP (Road Used as a Public Path) and cross some huge undulating fields on your way from Doddinghurst via Stondon Massey to ancient Blackmore. Part of the old plague route into the village is followed on your way to lunch. Try and plan this walk so you have time to have a look round the historic village of Blackmore. A large green, stocks and many old buildings will be found there. Continue to Wyatt's Green, followed by Peartree Green and then it's back to Doddinghurst and your car.

 *The Walk*

① From the village hall cross the road into the churchyard and make your way to the back, passing to the left of the church. You will find the footpath ahead. Walk with the rear of the gardens on your right till you come to a kissing gate and a footpath sign by house number 67 on the housing estate. Turn left and take the footpath signed before house 71; it has a fence on your right. You are about to enter **Church Wood** and make an interesting reverse half circle movement through it. Your progress is now almost regal and you soon have the luxury of the choice of a kissing gate or stile; then walk on a few steps to cross a wooden plank bridge. All the while you are likely to be serenaded by songbirds. You are making your way to the far edge of the wood, crossing another long plank bridge

as you go. A yellow arrow confirms you have to turn left. Walk with the edge of the wood on your right till you come to the next direction post, with a broken yellow arrow. You again turn left, and recross the wood, making your way over another wooden bridge to pass a pond, a further bridge, and more yellow arrows directing you gradually left. You are on your way to the far corner of the wood to turn right onto a footpath that runs along the rear of the gardens of some houses. This brings you to a squeeze gate and the footpath sign at the road. (1/2 mile)

*Doddinghurst was our home for about 10 years from 1968. The main road from the post office to the Moat pub, now neatly curbed and paved, was then edged by a mixture of hedges and grass verges. Mrs Watson's on the road to Wyatts Green was known far and wide as the place to get your groceries and catch up on the latest news. Old cyclists would at times appear and tell tales of coming here many years earlier at all hours to get their cooked breakfasts at the café she ran. The village school was housed in the building next door to the church. Today the village has grown; old holiday shacks have been pulled down and new houses built on each of their plots.*

② Turn right for a few feet till you find on your right another footpath sign and squeeze gate. Your way ahead is made all the more interesting as you pass some newly planted woods on your right. You are crossing what was a large field. Under the oak tree ahead you will find a waymark that guides you left to the right of the pond. The next yellow arrow indicates the route ahead is leftish towards another young wood. Through the other side you find a further yellow arrow and squeeze gate. Your onward route is now half left across an open field to the far end of the brick wall where the direction rightish is pointed out for you between the fences, up the drive and out to the road and footpath sign. Cross **School Road** with care, turning half left to go down the road opposite. As this road bends left, turn right by two upright concrete posts that mark the entrance to the RUPP. Follow this pleasant leafy lane, now purely for

the use of walkers, until you come to two further concrete posts. Just on your left you will see the recently renovated old **Soap House**, that it is said dates back to the late 1600s. Continue walking in the same direction. Ignore the footpath sign directly behind the **Soap House**. Make for the second one on your left, opposite **Danesfield**. It is marked by a footpath sign. (1 mile)

③ This cross-field path takes you over the slight brow of the hill and on a gentle slope down to **Stondon Massey**. You soon find a hedge on your right. Continue along this hedge line to the field corner where you turn right into a twitten beside a high wooden fence to the footpath sign and the road. Cross the road and walk beside the village pond. You may like to rest your weary bones here, or on the children's playing field if you have some young ones with you.

*Stondon Massey was the home of the great composer William Byrd, who lived at Stondon Place from 1593 to his death in 1623. The old church can be found about a mile north-west up the Ongar road.*

Once fully revived, walk on past **Soames Farm** to **Soames Mead**. On your right you will find a stile by a footpath sign; cross it and at the other side of this area of set-aside you find a further stile. Your route is straight on towards **Ashling's Farm**, which you can spot in the trees under the power lines. Cross the bridge when you reach it and walk with the hedge on your left to a further bridge. A yellow arrow points the way across a private road. (1 1/4 miles)

④ Head half left to a further yellow arrow and a path between big leylandi trees. Carry straight on through a gap and on again uphill across an enormous field to the end of a hedge to the right of some fir trees. A yellow arrow confirms you are on the right path and you walk at the rear of some gardens to a further yellow arrow. Turn right and walk beside a row of concrete posts to the footpath signs at the end of some chicken sheds. Turn right and head across a field to a direction post in front of bushes. Go straight on over the earth bridge, with a ditch on your left. At the next

yellow arrow turn right and walk with the ditch on your left. At the next yellow arrow cross over what was the ditch and walk with a hedge on your right. You get good views of the church ahead. Another ditch appears on your right. At the yellow and green waymark turn right to walk a few yards along the old plague route to the bungalow at the end of **Green Lane** and out to the road. Turn left and walk along this interesting **Blackmore village street** till you come to the roundabout, the old school, which is now a library, and the **Prince Albert** pub. (1 3/4 miles)

*Blackmore, set on the River Wid, was once the home of an Augustinian priory of twelve canons. Perhaps one of its best claims to fame is the fact that King Henry VIII liked to visit here incognito. Henry Fitzroy, his bastard son, was born here at the priory, Jericho. Church Street even today is a lovely place to wander, admire and imagine. The church is open to visitors on summer Sunday afternoons, and once a month teas are served in the grounds.*

**THE PRINCE ALBERT, BLACKMORE**

⑤ After lunch, walk on left into **Church Street**, passing the **Bull** inn, **Jericho** and many other old buildings on your way to the church. At the footpath sign go through the churchyard and cross the stile at the back. Walk straight on with the brick wall on your left. At the end of the wall walk on across a large open field with a clump of fir trees on your right to a concrete footpath sign opposite **Wenlock's Farm**. Walk left down the road to a wooden footpath sign and a very awkward stile beside a gate into the field on your right. A series of yellow arrows takes you to a pond, where you turn right over a bridge and stile to walk with a hedge on your left to a stile and high, planked wooden walkway, with a river on your left and another stile with a very big drop. Walk on with the hedge on your left to a stile and bridge at the yellow arrow. Walking rightish you are heading across a very large field to a tall post bridge and post. This is definitely one of the adventurous bits! Cross the next field out to the road, **Hay Green Lane**. Turn right and walk a few yards to the next concrete sign. Walk on across the field to the ditch; cross the earth bridge and walk right to the field corner with a ditch on your right, then turn left and continue along this field edge till you come to a gap into the **Ted Marriage playing field**. You have to cross to the far corner of this field but may well want to stop for rest – children may wish to use the play equipment or a picnic may be the order of the day. Head for the white railings and a grass track out to a kissing gate and the road. (2 miles)

⑥ Turn left and walk past **Wolves Farm** to **Pettits Lane**. Turn right into this lane and continue ahead till you come to **Brook Lane** on your right. It is marked 'no through lane access only'. As you proceed down **Brook Lane** it goes from a cinder track to a streamside path then back to a made up road again. Follow it right out to the **Doddinghurst** road. (1 1/2 miles)

⑦ Here you turn left uphill. Walk past the post office and on to **Peartree Green**. Just past **Peartree Farm** turn right into **Day's Lane** then right into **Dagwood Lane**. Turn right at the footpath sign and head diagonally half left across to the school. Follow the yellow arrows up beside the school into the village hall playing fields and back to your waiting car. (3/4 mile)

*Date walk completed:*

# GREAT SAMPFORD TO HELIONS BUMPSTEAD

**A NICELY THATCHED WELL**

**Distance:**
11³/₄ miles

**Map: OS Explorer 195 Braintree & Saffron Walden**

**Starting point:**
The Red Lion public
house in Great
Sampford.
GR 644354

**How to get there:** *Great Sampford is situated on the B1053
road between Braintree and Saffron Walden. Park in the road
in the vicinity of the Red Lion public house.*

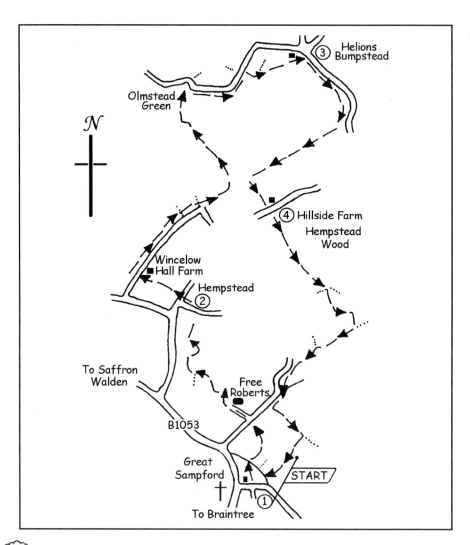

The **Three Horseshoes** in Helions Bumpstead has been known to us for many years. This 17th century pub is a traditional village pub that offers a warm welcome to locals and visitors alike. There is a sheltered garden for those warm sunny days where you can sit and sample the Greene King ales on offer. A good range of food is available, from bar snacks to full blown meals.

**Telephone:** *01440 730298.*

*This walk is over rolling countryside in the north-west corner of Essex, close to the border with Suffolk and Cambridgeshire. We start in the village of Great Sampford where there is much to see. It boasts a splendid church, a three-cornered grave, a large pond, and many houses of antiquity. One, called The How, still has its moat intact. Our route takes us on to Dick Turpin's Hempstead and finally to Helions Bumpstead – a fine little village with some excellent old timbered houses. The route is reasonably easy to follow and wide open skies are above as we travel to the pub at Helions Bumpstead for our lunch stop. The return route skirts Hempstead Wood and then heads south, along field paths and tracks, back to Great Sampford.*

 *The Walk*

*Great Sampford has many fine old houses. White House has ancient fireplaces and a handsome staircase. Tindon End, some way off to the south-west, has a panel with the date 1684, and some carved Tudor stones lying in the garden, but it is famous for another reason – it was the home for many years of John McAdam, the Scotsman who remade our English roads.*

① Just to the left of the **Red Lion** locate a footpath sign, number 24, between two fenced hedges and walk through into a playing field. Go over two stiles and soon cross another stile into an open field. Follow the telegraph lines to a stile leading across a byway onto a footpath. With a hedge on your left,

walk along this path, then continue on a wide path across an open field. At the end, turn left, following a yellow arrow to a road. Cross the road with a sign leading to **Free Roberts**. Pass the farmhouse and as you reach the farm buildings turn right at a byway sign. After 100 yards turn left at a T-junction towards a barn. Take a right turn north along a field edge with the hedge on your left and walk to the field corner. Turn left. Ignore a waymark to the left and turn right to climb up a field edge with the hedge on your left. At the top, turn right for a few yards, then turn left through a gap marked by an arrow. Now walk across a field to a projecting corner. Walk up with this field hedge on your right and go over a stile. Now head for a white cottage and join **Church Road**. Turn left on the road and enter the churchyard.
(2 miles)

*Hempstead is renowned for being the birthplace of Dick Turpin, the highwayman. He was born in the 17th-century inn and is known throughout the land for his wicked exploits. More to the credit of the village was William Harvey who, in the early 17th century, discovered how blood circulated round the body. He was buried in Hempstead in 1657.*

② Walk to the north of the church through a wide gap in the hedge and turn left downhill past the village hall to the road. Over to the right cross the road and enter a bridleway, heading up left through a wooded area. A steady climb leads to a moat which is the site of the old **Wincelow Hall**. Arrive at **Wincelow Hall Lane** and turn right along it. This long byway is, in various parts, a lane, a bridleway and a road used as a public footpath. It was once part of the main road to Bury St Edmunds. We will be content to cover a mile or so of it before our lunch stop and a similar amount from the other end later. Pass the present **Wincelow Hall** and **Great Dawkins Farm**. Now follow a path with a hedge on your left and at the end of the field you will see the rare sight of two red byway arrows. Turn left and follow the blue arrow signifying a public bridleway. The going is rougher now as the track drops to cross a stream and then climbs

towards **Olmstead Green**. Pass two blue arrows and soon bear right with a yellow arrow along a field edge over a bridge to a lane. Here the path should cross the road but, unless there has been serious clearance work since we walked there, that path is blocked. Instead, turn right and walk along the lane. Ignore a footpath sign in the corner but turn left and later right towards **Helions Farm** for 200 yards. Turn left to the left end of a wooded area and then right with a hedge on your right, aiming towards the church tower in the village ahead. Cross the drive and a stile downhill to walk along the field edge all the way to the side of the **Three Horseshoes** in **Helions Bumpstead**. (4 miles)

③ After a visit to the pub, turn right along **Water Lane**, passing a series of cottages. Finally, there is **End Cottage** and your walk is at the base of fields on either side. Pass **Newhouse Farm** and turn right to climb past **Boblow Hill Cottages** and reach the other end of the byway you were walking on earlier. The air is fresher here and at this height there are views to see. Pass the lane leading to **Boblow** and in a mile cross a ford. In 300 yards, turn left (with the hedge on your right) and walk all the way to the road. Just at the road you will have to force your way out of the field by a footpath sign. (2 miles)

④ Cross the road and enter **Ruses Farm**. Leave the track to the left, passing the left side of the farm buildings, then bear right back towards the end of the property to rejoin the track towards **Hempstead Wood**. You soon reach the wood and walk round the edge. Ignore the waymark and continue by the side of the wood. When the path turns left into the wood, turn right across the open field and make for the gap in the hedge on the far side of the field to turn right along the byway. Eventually take a sharp left and right turn and continue out to a lane. Turn left along the lane, passing **Jocelyns Farm** and **Sorrells Farm**. After **Monk's Farm** turn left at a footpath sign and follow the grass track, first on the left side of the hedge and later changing to the right side. The path crosses an earth bridge over a stream and immediately turns right along the bank of the stream. Later the path changes to the right bank and soon you reach **Spendring Lane South** at **Great Sampford**. Join the main road and walk along to the **Red Lion**. (3³/₄ miles)

*If you are not too tired, a visit to the church in Great Sampford is a must. Notice the two fierce goats standing out from the chapel*

THE THREE HORSESHOES, HELIONS BUMPSTEAD

gate, the niches in the buttresses, and the consecration crosses, formed of dark cut flint. The 14th-century tower has a stair turret of Tudor brick, and the nave has six fine columns supporting a 14th-century clerestory, in which a window was cut in the 15th-century to light the rood loft. There are roof beams, a porch, and a fine tomb recess, all 600 years old, and on an archway of the same time you will find some of the best carvings in Essex. One of the capitals has two monkey heads and rich foliage, while the other shows a cowled head, pigs with lolling tongues, and the head of an owl with its feathers delicately

suggested. There is a Tudor cupboard, a 17th-century chest and a beautiful six-sided table. The best modern craftsmanship is in the wooden lectern, a splendid eagle on rocks, with a pillar resting on lions. It is in memory of Robert Eustace, who died in 1905 after 55 years as vicar. We read his name again on a tiny cross in the shadow of the tower which marks the grave of his little child.

 Date walk completed:

# STEBBING TO GREAT BARDFIELD

**BRAZENHEAD FARM, PASSED ON THE ROUTE**

**Distance:**
12 miles

**Starting point:**
Stebbing village.
GR 662243

Map: OS Explorer 195 Braintree & Saffron Walden

**How to get there:** *Stebbing is situated about one mile to the north of the old Roman road running from Great Dunmow to Braintree and now known as the A120. It is easy to park on the main street, taking care of course not to obstruct any entrances and exits.*

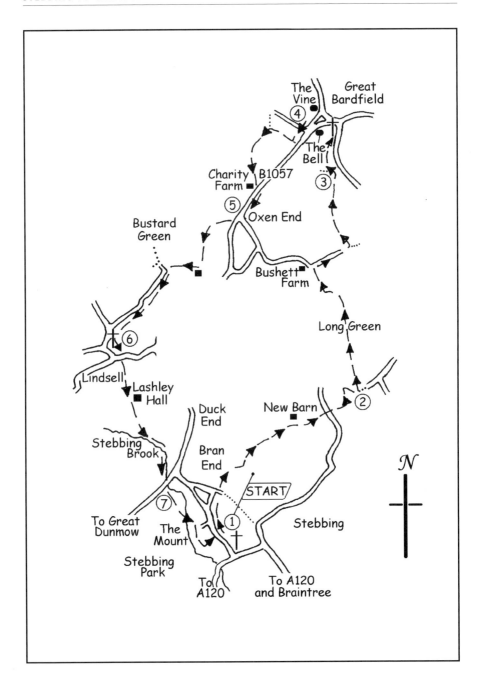

*S*tebbing and Great Bardfield are two of the very best villages in Essex. The start of the walk is largely by way of ancient tracks, almost totally unfettered by public roads of any description. The tracks are well used and easy to follow. The last mile to Great Bardfield church is along field edge paths and through a small wood. After lunch at the Vine, the route follows country lanes and discovers some quiet rural settlements. The lane leading from Bustard Green to Lindsell is a roadside nature reserve with scores of wildflowers on either side and you pass a beautiful pond, reminiscent at the right time of year of Monet's *Water Lilies*. From Lindsell churchyard we are led uphill to Lashley Hall and through the woods to the mill at Bran End. From here the route back to Stebbing is along broad water meadows. All in all, a delightful circuit.

The **Vine** at Great Bardfield is an inviting pub, with several bars and some lovely views over the village and its war memorial. There is a good range of drinks, and walkers should have no problem finding one of their favourite tipples. A blackboard menu displays the 'specials' of the day – we were lucky enough to sample the roast venison – and the usual bar snacks are also available.

**Telephone:** *01371 810355.*

## The Walk

*Stebbing is as old as the Domesday Book – the surrounding cottages and farms – at least 50 of them – are well over 300 years old. With its comfortable position a mile from any main road, one can certainly feel at ease in this beautiful village.*

① Walk north-west up the main village street. Follow a signpost to **Clay Lane** and come to a crossing track. Turn right and soon left (north) onto a track running north-east along the edge of a field. Pass a trig point and reach **New Bam**. At the right-hand side of the barn join another old byway and come to a road. Turn right along this and almost immediately left. Take a sharp turn to the left and then a sharp turn to the right. (2½ miles)

② Opposite a thatched cottage turn left on a narrow path leading to **Long Green**. You will reach a made up track, and should turn left towards **Bushett Farm**. Just before the farm buildings take the right-hand turn along a field edge with a hedge on your left. In the field corner turn left, following an arrow waymark by the hedge and follow the next field edge to reach a wood. Take the path through the wood to the end. (2¹/₂ miles)

③ Just before reaching the road turn left (north-west) for 50 yards.

Opposite a track on the left, turn right, keeping the fence on your left, and continue to the church. You may wish to have a look inside before exiting to the pavement by the road. Walk downhill to the village of **Great Bardfield**. Pass the butcher's shop and cross to the **Vine**. (³/₄ mile)

*Great Bardfield has very much the air of a small town rather than a village. In the past it had a market. Place House, at the top of the High Street, has an overhanging storey and was built*

THE VINE, GREAT BARDFIELD

*in 1564. In a window are the arms of the Bendlowes family and an inscription saying that William Bendlowes was a lawyer in the days of our two Tudor queens. His altar tomb is in the church, together with a brass portrait of his wife, and above is the remarkable chancel roof paid for by the Bendlowes family in 1618. The lowest part of the tower was built a few years before Magna Carta, and its small lead spire was added about the time of Queen Anne. The rest of the church is a very good example of 14th-century building, with handsome windows, a wonderful old door to let us in, and an impressive array of columns in the nave.*

④ After your refreshment stop, walk up the street till almost opposite the **Bell** public house to reach the beautiful old **Place House**. Here turn right for a hundred yards and then left at a footpath sign, passing the village hall, to reach a field. Turn right and left along a visible path to the field corner. Turn right past **Oyster Lake** and then turn left to follow **Black Lane** all the way to the road. Turn right along the road past **Charity Farm**. (1³/₄ miles)

⑤ At the sign to **Oxen End** turn right opposite **The Cottage** and follow the field edge to a bridge. Cross the bridge to a waymark. Turn left and go past a wood. As you

reach the first thatched cottage at **Brazenhead Farm**, turn right along a wide track and follow this to a little road called **Daisylea Road**. This has been designated a roadside nature reserve, and as you turn left along this during spring and summer you will find that the verges are a mass of wildflowers. At a kink in the road there is a delightful lily pond on the left – Monet eat your heart out! On reaching a slightly larger road turn left for 50 yards. When the road turns sharply to the right, go left on a path which leads into **Lindsell** churchyard. (2 miles)

*Many years ago the local pub was closed and nowadays there is little traffic through this tucked-away village. Bustard Green and Gallows Green are two of its outlying hamlets, and the tiny village centre is at Church Green. This, then, is Lindsell – a lovely place to discover.*

⑥ A visit inside the little church is a must, to savour the simple beauty. When you are ready, leave the churchyard to the south-east and, keeping the buildings to your right, arrive at a road. Turn right. As you reach the first cottage on your left there is a footpath post and a slight gap in the hedge. Go through this between a fence on the left and a shed to walk along the garden and cross a stile at the bottom. Go through the trees for a few yards and come to an arable field. Keep the field boundary on your right at first. Cross to the other side of the hedge after 50 yards, now walking with the hedge on your left. At the top of the little hill you reach the barns at **Lashley Hall** and continue between them. Take the track to the south and when you reach a facing hedge turn left to join another track. Here turn right downhill for 20 yards. Do not continue into the wood but turn left along the field edge to the end of rough ground on your right. Turn right and then left before a field division. Now look carefully to your right as you approach a wood to spot and walk to a bridge over rough ground. You find, in fact, two bridges together. Cross the bridge on the right and follow this path along the edge of the wood by the side of the river to

**Tanner's Farm**. Continue on this route to cross the road to the mill. (1½ miles)

⑦ Climb over a stile and make your way along wide water meadows, over a stream to a gap in the hedge and on to the gates of **Stebbing Park**. Cross the estate drive and walk down towards the huge mound which was the base for a moated Norman castle. From the narrow path outside a fence, go through a gate into the cricket ground, pass the United Reformed church and return to the **High Street**. (1 mile)

*Date walk completed:*

# HYLANDS PARK TO EDNEY COMMON

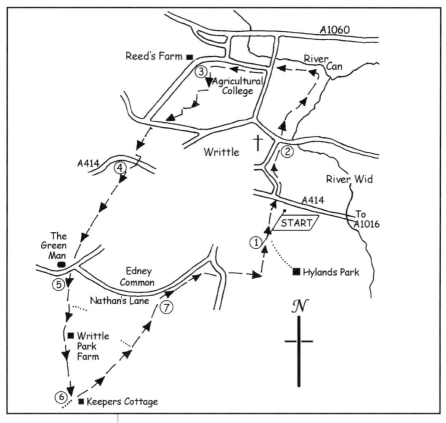

**Distance:**
10¹/₄ miles

**Starting point:**
Hylands Park.
GR 680048

**Map: OS Explorer 183 Chelmsford & The Rodings**

**How to get there:** *Hylands Park lies just south-west of Chelmsford. Take the A414 west out of town and you will find the park entrance clearly signed about 1 mile west of the Widford roundabout. Go up the drive through the metal entrance gates and at the fork turn right to park near the toilet block in the park.*

SHEEP ENJOY THE PASTURES OF WRITTLE AGRICULTURAL COLLEGE

*T*his fairly flat, rural walk near the county town of Chelmsford begins in Hylands Park, open from 7.30 am to dusk. The route then passes through historic Writtle and near the site of Marconi's first radio broadcasts. A long green lane brings you north to the River Can. An interesting section follows though the grounds of Writtle Agricultural College and round the back of Great Oxney Green. Then the fields get bigger and the views wider as you make your way south-east over the A414 to Edney Common. After lunch, one of the longer, more hilly sections takes you along a fine concrete track with wide downhill views deep into the valley. A lovely series of woods follows before you start to climb and have a chance to enjoy the birds that seem to rejoice that you have come to visit them. Back on the road east of Edney Common there is a chance to rest your navigation finger as an easy walk brings you north and east to a very pretty permissive path and a short cut back into Hylands Park.

The **Green Man** at Edney Common is a traditional rural pub that offers a warm welcome. There is plenty of space to sit and relax, and, in fine weather, you can take advantage of the large garden. The inn has a fully carpeted bar and restaurant area. The beers on offer are Greene King IPA and John Smith's Smooth, alongside Guinness, and Foster's and Heineken lagers. The bar snacks include soup, jacket potatoes and sandwiches with salad. An excellent platter of ham, egg and chips is among the hot dishes available.

**Telephone:** *01245 248076.*

① With your back to the toilet block, walk ahead through the gap in the railings at the permissive path sign and bear right through the woods towards the park entrance, bypassing the iron gates to come out on the road by the A414 underpass. Turn left and go down the underpass, noting the plaque.

*The plaque tells you this is a Commemorative Walk with no less than 100 oaks having been planted to mark the passing of 50 years since the end of the Second World War.*

Ignoring the footpath sign on your right, continue to the T-junction at **Paradise Road** and follow the centenary circle waymark, turning right. (1 mile)

*Writtle was in existence in Roman times and two Roman burial urns have been found in the old vicarage gardens. In the Domesday Book of 1086, Writtle was recorded as having a population of 500 and being the largest parish in the county. It was a royal manor belonging to King William and once a favourite haunt of King John who built his hunting lodge in 1211 in the grounds of today's Writtle College. The whole village is riddled with interesting history, including the intriguing underground canal system. You may have time to walk up to the green (left past Barclays Bank) to have a quick look at some of the lovely buildings before returning to your walk.*

② Passing **Barclays Bank** and the **Cock and Bell** pub, cross the road. Go straight across into **St John's Green**. At the yellow arrow turn right into **Lawford Lane** and walk past **Melba Court**, where you will find the Marconi memorial notice. Retrace a step or two and make for the farm gate. Follow the centenary circle down **Lawford Lane**, which has, by this time, reverted to the green lane it was in the days of King John.

*Guglielmo Marconi, born in 1874, made his first regular radio broadcasts in early 1920 from a hut that used to stand near here. He used the call sign 'Two Emma Toc' (2MT). Lawford Lane is part of the ancient route used by travellers on their way between London and East Anglia. Those wanting to cross the River Can and avoid the impassable marshy area near Chelmsford came this way. This was, of course, before Bishop Maurice of London built the bridge in Chelmsford in 1101.*

When you come to the **River Can**, turn left and go through the gap in a wooden fence to walk west, with the river on your right, all the way out to the road by a footpath sign. Turn left, and then right into **Cow-watering Lane**. You walk for just over 1/2 mile along the lane till you come to **Reed's Farm**, all the while passing college grounds on your left. (2 1/4 miles)

*Writtle Agricultural College holds open days when you can see some of the excellent displays near the administration buildings, where groups of students have worked to create small garden areas with a theme. There are also areas in the college grounds where livestock are farmed and fruit grown to commercial standards. The farm shop just down the road from the crossing at point 2 is open to the public and is another window into their activities.*

③ Turn left at the wooden footpath sign and take the hedged path into the college grounds. You will soon see fine examples of fruit growing and arable farming. Walk with the hedge on your left to the estate road. A yellow arrow confirms your route is ahead, down a dip, with vegetation on the right, to a brook. Turn right onto **Sturgeons Walk**. A direction post and yellow arrow confirm the way. Turn left and go across a concrete bridge over the brook and walk between two wire fences. You have now entered the livestock area of the college grounds and are walking round a reservoir. At the yellow arrow turn right and before the gate right again (**Daws Walk**). You are walking along the base of the reservoir now, with hedge on your left. You soon come to a stile and enter a woodland canopy. At the T-junction turn left and just as the houses come into view one field away turn right and walk along the track out to the road. Turn right for a short road walk. Two fields after **Clovers** turn left at a concrete footpath sign and cross the bridge, walking ahead with the hedge on your left. Cross the next wooden bridge and walk under the overhead power lines, continuing to the layby beside the A414. There is a direction post to confirm you have arrived at the right place. (1½ miles)

④ Cross the A414 and walk left along the old road till you come to some houses. Turn right at the footpath sign beside the conifers. Go through the gap and then cross the field to a high waymark that marks the bridge over the stream. Turn left and walk with the stream on your left. Ignore the concrete bridge and continue ahead till you come to the corner of **Lady Grove**. Cross the wooden bridge and turn right, to walk with the wood on your right. This is an ideal spot for a picnic if you have brought your own food along. At the next bridge, go straight on over the track and walk with a hedge on your right, passing a yellow arrow. At the next yellow arrow, bear slightly right and go through the gap, over the wooden bridge and walk with a ditch on your left. As the field goes right,

**THE GREEN MAN, EDNEY COMMON**

watch for the yellow arrow just past the bend that indicates you turn left. Here you walk down a lovely grassy track to a kissing gate direction post and the road. Turn right and past the houses you will find the **Green Man** pub on your right. (1 1/2 miles)

⑤ After lunch, retrace your steps some 20 yards to take the bridleway on the right going south. At first it looks like a minor road and you follow this south, ignoring a left turn and footpaths on both the right and left. Walk past the road signs 'No Through Road' and 'Road Closed' to pass **Writtle Park Farm** and continue into **Writtle Park**. You will pass several farm buildings and workers' cottages to take the right concrete road round the entrance to **Writtle Park Farm**. Now there follows just under a mile of gentle descent on a quiet private road with wonderful wide views over **Wells and Sheds Farm** towards Fryerning. (1 1/4 miles)

⑥ As the road flattens out, look for a left turn just before **Keepers Cottage**. Take the route indicated by the arrows, uphill on a track which can be muddy at times. It bends right then left as you continue a gentle ascent, working hard to regain the height you so willingly lost on the way down. Many areas of the woods here have been lovingly coppiced in recent years.

Follow the track to the end of the wood where you will find a yellow arrow indicating you have to turn right. A few yards further on you come to a three-way arrow and your route turns right into the undergrowth under a very tall dead tree. You soon emerge into a large grassy field. Follow the direction indicated by the footpath sign down the left-hand side of the field. About halfway down at a yellow arrow, turn diagonally right. If you look over your right shoulder, you should be just level with the radio towers. Continue straight across the heath on a well-walked path to reach another footpath sign. You are about to enter the next wood. Cross two bridges and follow the direction post when it tells you to go left. You are heading for the right-hand corner of **Great Edney Wood** and the exit into **Nathan's Lane**. (1 1/4 miles)

⑦ Turn right for a road walk of about 3/4 mile, first down **Nathan's Lane**, then right onto busy **Margaretting Road**. Fortunately just round the first bend on your left you will find a permissive path. It is marked with a wooden footpath sign and **Mascalls**. Follow the cinder track down to the gate and continue to the woods. When among the trees, follow the main track in a roughly easterly direction. At the far side of the woods you are back in **Hylands Park**. Turn left and walk with the woodland on your left all the way back to your car. The park is an excellent place to enjoy a picnic tea if you have packed one. (1½ miles)

*Chelmsford Council has owned Hylands Park since 1966. The house was built in 1730 for Sir John Comyns, MP for Maldon. Later owners added wings and the fine portico, also an additional storey in about 1840. The building has now been restored and the Victorian top storey removed. It is said to appear today much as it did between 1820 and 1835 and is well worth a visit. Teas are offered at the house on summer Sunday afternoons and the cakes are delightful. The park, which includes the beautiful garden, is open to the public every day except for two weekends in August when music festivals are held. We would recommend that you choose to do this walk on any day of the year except over these two long weekends. If, however, you find this is the only time you can manage, take your car to the free public car park in Writtle and start and end the walk at point 2. Ring 01245 606812 for further information on events at Hylands House.*

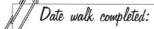

Date walk completed:

# SOUTH HANNINGFIELD TO RAMSDEN BELLHOUSE

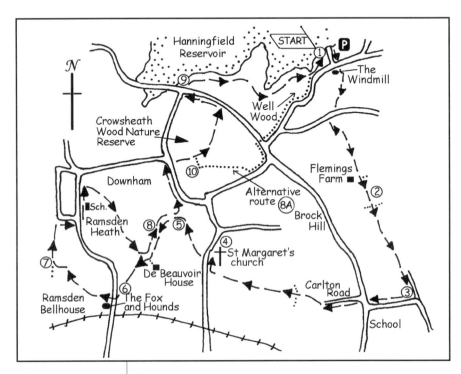

**Distance:**
9¹/₂ miles

**Starting point:**
The visitor's car park at Hanningfield Reservoir.
GR 737977

**Map: OS Explorer 175 Southend-on-Sea & Basildon**

**How to get there:** South Hanningfield lies approximately 1 mile west of the new A130 and about 1¹/₂ miles west of Rettendon. From the old A130, take the country lane opposite the Rettendon Bell pub, South Hanningfield Road, and drive west (under the new A130 road) to South Hanningfield. Just after the Windmill pub, turn right down Giffords Lane to the Hanningfield Reservoir visitors' car park. This is open from 9 am to 4 pm (3 pm in winter). If you are timing your walk to return later than this, you can leave your car near the reservoir at GR 742978.

THE VISITOR CENTRE AT HANNINGFIELD RESERVOIR

*T*his is perhaps the most challenging walk in the book, with plenty of stiles and a few taxing climbs. However, you will be amply rewarded with many fine views, some interesting buildings, and a warm welcome at a fine pub. Setting off from Hanningfield Reservoir, a rolling cross-field path brings you to the outskirts of Runwell. Passing through Downham, with its delightful church perched on a steep hillside, there begins a series of ups and downs before you arrive in Ramsden Bellhouse for a lunchtime stop. The return route gives you the opportunity to visit the wonderful Essex Wildlife Trust reserves located alongside the reservoir. However, please note that they are normally closed on Mondays (except bank holidays). An alternative route back from Crowsheath Wood, omitting the reserves, is also described.

The interesting **Fox and Hounds** at Ramsden Bellhouse was erected in 1927 to serve travellers at the proposed railway station nearby. However, the station was never built. The old pub it replaced became the Foxes, a private house. The Fox and Hounds is a lively hostelry, with oak beams, a long bar and a piano. There is a separate, very popular, restaurant. The choice of beers includes Long Willey, Good Old Boy, Ridleys IPA and Crouch Vale Best. You might well find other guest beers. The regular weekday menu includes such dishes as lasagne, steak and kidney pie, curry, chilli con carne and burgers. A traditional Sunday roast is served, and children's meals and a 'Big Breakfast' are available. There is also a good selection of bar snacks.

**Telephone:** *01268 710286.*

# The Walk

① Having spent a few minutes admiring the setting, walk back along **Giffords Lane**. At the road, turn left and walk down the dip and up to the car park of the **Windmill** public house on your right, passing a footpath sign. Make for the footpath at the rear left-hand corner of the car park. Cross the stile and climb uphill with a hedge on your left. At the yellow arrow marker, turn right under the wires and continue to climb. When you come to the dung heap go right and left, and continue with the hedge on your left to some gates; cross the nearby stile, passing a footpath sign, to arrive at a road, Turn right along **Warren Road** and left beside the next footpath sign to climb over (you have guessed it) another stile and go round to the rear of a small

reservoir. This brings you back onto your southerly path. You will find yourself walking beside a wire fence on the right of the reservoir. At the yellow arrow marker, continue straight ahead across a field to the far corner of the next field. Now pop through an old gate entrance on your right and continue in a southerly direction with the hedge on your left. In the dip slightly to your right you will see beautiful **Flemings Farm**. (1 mile)

*We are sure Flemings Farm will thrill you as it does us. Its lovely Elizabethan wing still stands. Sir Edmund Sulyard was one of the people who lived here. When he died in 1692, he was buried in nearby Runwell church.*

② The path goes through a gap in the hedge ahead. Ignore the yellow arrows to the path on your left and carry straight on downhill, with the hedge on your right, as far as the stile, which you cross. Follow the direction of the arrow south uphill. You may be able to pick up the faint track on the ground. When you reach the top, adjust your walking line to aim downhill for a bridge in the valley ahead. There is a crossing path here, just before the stile and bridge which you cross. Keep straight on with the hedge on your left. As the field end curls round right, take the second bridge on your left. You will then see a hedge with a ditch behind it on your left. Continue in a southerly direction till you come to a cottage on your left. Go over the stile and the track ahead becomes a road, **South Hanningfield Way**. (1¹/₄ miles)

③ At house number 92, turn right passing number 94. Continue down the road until you arrive at a roundabout. Turn right into **Brock Hill**, then, several roads later, left into **Carlton Road**. At the T-junction, **Station Road**, turn right to a footpath sign and stile. Head slightly left to a stile which is just right of the left-hand corner of the field. Cross the stile and pick up an old road. Walk left uphill to the footpath signs. As the track goes right, you should go straight on through a gap in the hedge to enter a grassy field, following footpath sign 18. You now get your first glimpse of **Downham church** at the top of the hill. This may be a good

place to stop for a picnic or have a short rest. Walk on with the hedge on your right, to admire **Downham Hall**, a pretty pink, timbered house, half left ahead. Go through the gap in front of you, along a well-walked narrow path under power lines, crossing a stile and bridge. Go straight on over a field to a yellow arrow marker and then across a second open field to another stile, bridge and stile. Continue in the same direction over a third open field to a yellow arrow marker, which directs you to the right of a pond. The next stretch can be muddy. You are now heading for a stile on your left, then to the right of a farmhouse and the stile behind it. Follow the yellow marker and turn left down the drive to the road and footpath sign. Turn right uphill on the road to **St Margaret's church**, Downham, where you may wish to have a rest and look round the grounds, admiring the unusual outbuilding with a dovecote. (1¹/₂ miles)

④ Your onward route crosses the road, making for a stile. Head half right just to the left of a water trough on a faint path over the crest of the hill. Proceed downhill to the stile, pausing to take in the lovely view spread before you. Go over the stile. Your way is now along a path climbing with a hedge on your right. When you come to the permissive footpath sign, follow it round the edge of the field (it is a lot easier than the unwalked cross-field path). Cross over the next stile and turn left. (¹/₄ mile)

⑤ Walk with the hedge on your left to the field and then pop through a gap with a yellow waymark and go left downhill, passing caravans and outbuildings, and through the woods to a stile in the left-hand corner. Cross two further stiles and pass to the left of a house with friendly dogs. Walk on through the farmstead, with its collection of telephone boxes, to cross two further stiles to the right of the

drive. Turn right along an unmade road. Cross over the second stile on the left into an open field and head for another stile in the far corner, just to the left of a large black barn. Walk down the gravel drive and through the gate to find a footpath sign and the road. Turn left. Just past the bus stop on your right, you will find the very welcoming **Fox and Hounds** pub. (1 mile)

⑥ After lunch, retrace your steps and, just before the bus stop, turn left up **Chase Bungalow** drive. Go through two gates. Beside the third gate, turn right and take the fenced

THE FOX AND HOUNDS, RAMSDEN BELLHOUSE

area uphill on a rough path between paddocks to a stile on your right. Cross it and continue uphill to a yellow arrow marker; go over the next stile and up to another fence. After this fence continue straight ahead to a stile in the corner of the field, marked with a yellow arrow. Walk straight on with the hedge on your left to a stile on the left. Go over the stile and through a paddock, which can be muddy at times, to a series of gates opposite. Go through two gates to the footpath sign by the road near the Hillbrow sign. (³/₄ mile)

⑦ Turn right. There now follows a road walk to let you regain your strength. Follow this road all the way to the junction of **Park Lane** with **Short Lane**. Turn right and walk to the T-junction. Turn left and walk past the primary school to house number 19. Look for the concrete public footpath sign and go right down a fenced path to a stile. Carry straight on to the next gap in the hedge with the hedge on your left. Now head half right to a stile hidden under an arch of trees. Cross the stile and turn right, walking with a wire fence and some trees on your right. Ignore a yellow arrow and stile into the woods on your right. Instead, continue ahead, admiring the views to **Downham church** till you come to a stile in the corner of the field. Turn left on a cross-field path in the direction of the church. At the stile turn right and walk to the next stile and bridge. Turn left on the farm road to pass a bridleway sign. Between **De Beauvoir Lodge** and **De Beauvoir House** turn left uphill to retrace your route over the five stiles and back up through the woods to the yellow arrow marker. (1³/₄ miles)

⑧ Turn right and walk with a hedge on your right to a footpath sign at the corner of the field. Turn left and walk with a hedge on the right to a gate by the footpath sign with a yellow butterfly. At the seat, turn left and walk through the pretty **Queen's Silver Jubilee gardens**. Go left along the road, passing a pond and the village hall. Just before the road turns left, turn right at a concrete footpath post, walking on a narrow path with a hedge on your left and a fence on your right. You soon come to a stile and an entrance to **Crowsheath Wood Nature Reserve** run by Essex Wildlife Trust. If the reserve is closed, you will need to take the alternative route back to the start of the walk which is indicated at point 8A (see below and on the sketch map). Otherwise, carry on by crossing the stile and following the path round the edge of the wood. Turn left, passing a stile and then walking with the fence on your left. Soon you will pass a very smart bungalow on your right. When you reach the gate, turn left and walk down the road to the entrance to the Essex Wildlife Trust **Hanningfield Reserve**. (1 mile)

*Hanningfield Reservoir covers 874 acres. In the early days the flies that bred on this still water became such a nuisance to the villagers living nearby that the water engineers stocked the reservoir with fish, which ate the flies. Then the water authorities issued licences, at no small cost, to come and catch the well-fed fish. A cycle that reaped satisfactory rewards all round.*

⑨ Head for the visitor centre where you may wish to stop awhile. Leave by the rear of the centre and take the main path through the reserve, keeping between the water's edge and the fence on your right. The main path goes out right to the fence with a field on your right. Pass a pond and come to a junction of paths, then turn right to pass a seat and a large number 8. You then go ahead, passing numbers 3, 2 and 1. When you come to another 8 ignore the Hawkwood Trail on your right and turn left. At **Well Wood** take another left. Now follows a gentle

loop towards the water's edge and back. When you approach the letter A and fire beaters, turn left to go over the bridge and on to the fisherman's lodge and your waiting car. The more adventurous amongst you may wish to make a short detour to visit one of the interesting bird hides on your way from the visitor centre. (1 mile)

⑧Ⓐ **Alternative route:** From the stile near **Crowsheath Wood Nature Reserve**, turn right following the yellow arrow markers on a cross-field path. The route takes you left, then parallel with the road before you turn right through a gap in the hedge to **Sudbury Road**. Turn left to start a road walk of about a mile in total. Arrive at a T-junction, then go left for a few yards to the next right turn, into **South Hanningfield Road**. You will find yourself walking outside **Well Wood** and the nature reserve as you make your way back to your car. Your total route is still 9$\frac{1}{2}$ miles because what you lose in the reserve you make up for on the road.

*Date walk completed:*

# PAPER MILL LOCK
# TO HATFIELD PEVEREL

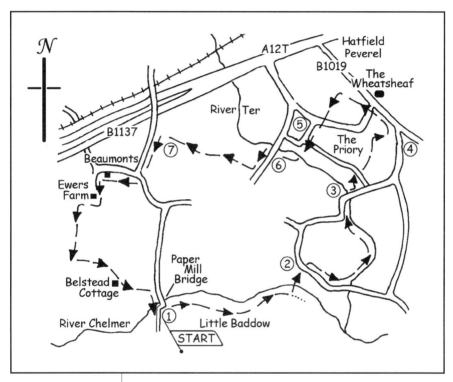

**Distance:**
8 miles

Map: OS Explorer 183 Chelmsford & The Rodings

**Starting point:**
Paper Mill Lock on
the Chelmer and
Blackwater
Navigation.
GR 776089

**How to get there:** *Paper Mill Lock lies on the banks of the
Chelmer and Blackwater Navigation where it is crossed by the
road running north from the A414 in Danbury through Little
Baddow to the B1137 on the outskirts of Hatfield Peverel.
Park beside the road on the south side of the canal.*

BRIDGE OVER THE CHELMER AND BLACKWATER NAVIGATION

*T*his is one of our favourite circuits, particularly in summer. It is a largely waterside walk that starts in the valley bottom. The route follows the wide bank of the canal to cross the water on an old footbridge. After a stroll along a country lane you meet the tiny River Ter at Bumfords Bridge, and things get more exciting as you hug its banks on a winding course. At the ford, you cross the river and head north, climbing along a series of back ways to pass through Nounsley and reach Hatfield Peverel. After a well-earned rest, the return journey takes you through this pleasant village and you start to descend, with some lovely wide views back down to the Ter, and then another stretch of the riverbank brings you to Long Wood. You walk gently downhill through fields into the Chelmer valley again to reach the canal at Paper Mill Lock.

The **Wheatsheaf** at Hatfield Peverel is a friendly village local that lies slightly back from the B1019 Maldon road. We suggest you make your way into the pub via the rear garden, passing the large aviary on the way. It houses a wonderful collection of brightly coloured birds like cockatiels. On the other side of the path is a small cage for a family of lively chipmunks. The whole is surrounded by ranks of picnic tables. Inside, the blackboard over the fireplace displays a selection of delicious home-made food which might include steak pies, curries, pasta and vegetarian dishes. There is a tempting pudding menu, also a wide choice of bar snacks. Ridleys ales are served here.

**Telephone:** *01245 380330.*

 *The Walk*

*Paper Mill Lock lies in a wonderful situation on the valley floor, with the road descending to reach it from both north and south. When you arrive you will find the canal, a busy weir and the thriving business that is Chelmer Cruises. The good barge 'Victoria' makes her way along the canal, with a regular cargo of willing tourists throughout the summer season. Young people enjoy learning to canoe here and fishermen try their hand at a more relaxing form of sport.*

① Make your way to the south side of the road bridge and go through the little gate by the public footpath sign displaying a yellow butterfly. This takes you onto the canal side footpath. Head north-east along this wide and, at times, shady path as

the navigation sweeps right and left. Just as it turns right again you will spot a footbridge. Turn left over the concrete bridge with white railings, noting it was built in 1951. Walk right and left, then follow a well-used path to cross a field to a remote country lane hidden behind a row of willow trees by a footpath sign. Funny this, since what you have just walked up is shown as a bridleway on the OS map! (1 mile)

*The River Chelmer and its many tributaries is the principal river of Essex. It runs from its source near Debden to be just beaten into the sea at Heybridge by the slightly longer Blackwater River. In the 1790s it was made navigable from Chelmsford to Maldon and this stretch was named the Chelmer and Blackwater Navigation. It was used for transporting cargo for many years until the railways took over as the main route for goods traffic. It is still used for pleasure purposes and, in the summer, you will see a parade of colourful boats making their way along the canal.*

② You have now reached **Bumfords Lane** and should turn right (south-east), passing a sign indicating that cars may wobble! Stroll along this pleasant country route for about 500 yards until you reach a bridge. Just before the bridge, which is but a three strand wooden structure each side of the road, turn left to walk in a northerly direction on the left-hand side of the little **River Ter**. Your way ahead follows the shape of a lazy 'S', bending first right, then left, then right again. Just as you think it is going on forever, you come to a ford. For those of you carrying a picnic this could be the place to enjoy it. (1½ miles)

③ Cross the ford, using the footbridge, if necessary, to avoid getting your feet wet. Follow the road round a right-hand bend, pass a few houses at the start of **Nounsley** village and start looking for a twitten on your left. You will find it beside a yellow hydrant marker and it is marked by a public footpath sign. Take this fenced path, climbing gently uphill. The road you are approaching is **Sportsmans Lane** and the **Sportman's Arms** pub is down on your left. However, there is a little further to go before your lunch break. Turn a few steps right, then immediately left, beside a public footpath sign. This path

THE WHEATSHEAF, HATFIELD PEVEREL

continues with a hedge and fence on your left. You are climbing now towards **Hatfield Peverel**. Ignore two paths off to your right and continue ahead, passing the **Priory** on your left. If you go through the iron gates and across the grounds, you can walk half left towards the **Priory church** and get a closer view of this fine old building. Retrace your steps to the iron gate, turn left and then, as you approach the housing estate, turn right round the edge of some allotments. Go down between the houses to come out on the road. ($1/_2$ mile)

*The Priory was established in the 12th century by William Peverel. His mother Ingelrica, the daughter of a noble Saxon, became the mistress of William the Conqueror. She later married Ralph Peverel and, regretting in her old age her past behaviour, she founded a college for secular canons. Her son converted the college into a Benedictine priory and endowed it further.*

④ Now follows a road walk to the **Wheatsheaf** pub. Turn left and the side road you are on is joined from your right by the B1019. Keep left here. Cross the road with care to your lunch stop. After your visit to the pub, cross the road again and take the path in a gap opposite, between two houses. Cross the road and go through another footpath

opening to the right of the infant school. This brings you out onto the village playing fields. Join a fairly new tarmac track heading up the left-hand side of the playing fields to a well-walked path, taking you to the right of a pond and onto a housing estate. Turn left down **Laburnum Way**, then right at the crossroads into **Willow Crescent**. After passing a few houses, look for a twitten on your left, just after house number 10. Go down the twitten, cross the next estate road and take a second twitten south. (1 mile)

*Have you emerged intact from the village? Hatfield Peverel is famous for its witches. At the assizes in Chelmsford in 1566 Elizabeth Francis, Mother Agnes Waterhouse and her daughter Joan were questioned by lawyers and judged to have powers vested in them by the Devil. So seriously did they take these findings that Mother Waterhouse was hanged.*

⑤ You have now reached the hut used by the Hatfield Peverel Scouts and Guides. Look for the footpath sign that leads to either a stile or a kissing gate in the rear fence. Cross to the right-hand corner of the field ahead, with allotments on your right; head south-west downhill to **Sportsmans Lane**. When you reach the lane, continue in the same direction for 150 yards, passing

**Gregories**, and come to another path. Carry on in the same direction, with a hedge on your right, till you come to a long concrete footbridge over the **River Ter** – another possible picnic venue. ($1/2$ mile)

*The River Ter rises near Stebbing and flows south to join the Chelmer just south of Bumfords Lane.*

⑥ Turn right and walk along the bank of the Ter to reach the road at the red-brick **Crabbs Bridge**. Turn left and walk uphill till you spot a footpath sign hidden in a bush on your right. This field edge path takes you across the field, with the hedge on your left, then alongside **Long Wood**, first with it on your left, then on your right. Cross a track and continue ahead under some power lines with the wood then a ditch on your right. Finish along the side of a field and come out onto the road. (1 mile).

⑦ Turn left and walk down **Mowden Hall Lane**. There are good views over to your left. Take the next lane to the right; there is normally a notice about produce for sale just as you turn the corner. In about 400 yards pass a pond then, just round the bend, come to a footpath on your left at a house called **Beaumonts**. Take the opening to the right of the gatepost. The way you need to go is along a track to the right of **Beaumonts** as far as **Ewers**, passing a farm gate. Pass what appear to be stable buildings, following the main track right down to the old **Ewers farm building**. Go ahead under the wooden arch into the garden, passing just to the left of the cottage, and make your way down to the bridge at the end of the garden. The yellow arrow confirms your route is right at the bridge. Walk with the stream on your right to a post. Turn left to cross a large arable field. You are heading at an angle of 90° from the stream, slightly uphill to a waymark post. Continue ahead at the yellow arrow with the hedge on your right until you come to a footpath post. At the junction with a crossing track, turn left. We always want to stop along here and soak up the view. This wide firm track brings you gently downhill past **Belstead Cottages** back to the road. You are just yards from **Paper Mill Lock** and your car. ($2^1/2$ miles)

*Date walk completed:*

# TERLING TO WHITE NOTLEY

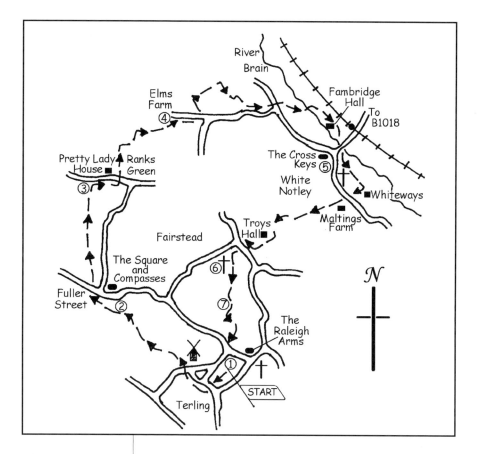

**Distance:**
11 miles

**Starting point:**
The village hall in Terling.
GR 772151

Map: OS Explorer 183 Chelmsford & The Rodings

**How to get there:** From the A12 between Chelmsford and Colchester, follow the signs to Hatfield Peverel. The road to the station is also signposted to Terling. Turn left in the centre of Terling and continue to the village hall. Park on the opposite side of the track.

*T*he seemingly simple country village of Terling conceals a rather grand past. Henry VIII had a palace here and, in Victorian times, Terling Place was home to the third Lord Rayleigh, regarded as the most learned man who ever lived in England. This walk takes you through exceptionally pretty countryside. It climbs towards Terling windmill, then drops to the level of the River Ter before rising to Fuller Street. Then it is over farmland to Queens Wood, and on to the hamlet of Ranks Green. There is the opportunity to stop for lunch at the historic village of White Notley before returning to Terling along gentle valley paths.

The **Cross Keys** in Notley is a welcoming little pub in the heart of the village. The food is varied and is available lunchtime (except Monday) and evening. You will find all the rambler's favourites – sausage, egg and chips, jacket potatoes, baguettes and sandwiches. The pub is closed, though, at lunchtime on Monday. There are two real ales on offer including Ridleys IPA and another, often Rumpus.

**Telephone:** *01376 583297.*

*The Walk*

① Walk past the village hall and up a track, passing the village swimming pool and tennis courts.

*For nearly half a century, Lord Rayleigh carried out his work of scientific discovery in Terling, and he was awarded the Nobel prize in 1904. When in 1825 one of his predecessors needed a sort of overspill to accommodate guests, he built what is now the village*

*pub – the Rayleigh Arms, of course.*

Continue through a gate to reach the cricket ground. Pass another gate to walk to a road. Turn right to go clockwise round **Flack's Green**, a small green. Turn left along **Hull Road** and turn right by a red telephone box into **Oakfield Lane**. Keep to the right of a hedge into a field by a yellow arrow waymark. At the corner of the hedge on your left continue in the same direction, crossing the field to a stile and later going left through a gate opening.

The path leads to a metal gate with a stile at the side. Follow the path round to the left and continue on a grassy track between an avenue of young willow trees. Keep on along a path which can be wet at times and at the end turn right to cross a rather rough field by a bridge over the **River Ter**; go uphill to a track. Turn left along this track and go between thick bushy hedges. Turn left along the field and right at the end to reach a road by a footpath sign. (1 1/2 miles)

**BARNS NEAR FAMBRIDGE HALL**

② Turn left and pass the **Square and Compasses** at **Fuller Street**, walking along the road signposted to **Great Leighs**. At a bend turn right by a footpath sign into a field. By the side of the field there is a comfortable wide grassy path which leads to a fine pond built in the last ten years or so for fishing and irrigation. Later, the path deteriorates but at the field corner, turn right over a plank bridge into the adjacent field. Turn left for 100 yards to enter Queen's Wood. Immediately cross a stile and follow a wide ride leading north through the wood. You will find only one waymark but keep the edge of the wood in sight 50 yards to the right. Finally the path turns right to a stile

by a field. Cross this and turn left. Cross a metal stile. Soon look on your left for another metal stile and cross back into the trees. Follow the path and go over a plank bridge by a waymark. In 100 yards you will reach a country lane at **Ranks Green**. (1 1/2 miles)

③ Turn right and walk on for 400 yards, passing a former pub, alas closed several years ago. It had the marvellous name of the Pretty Lady, which is preserved in the name of the dwelling – **Pretty Lady House**. Soon you will reach a row of houses; look carefully for a concrete public footpath sign and turn left up a grassy path leading between houses to arable fields at the back. The path continues on the field edge for 200 yards. Turn left by a waymark to walk round the next field. Turn left through a gap and cross the field to a waymark post at the left end of a hedge. Do not go straight on but turn right for 50 yards, now turning left with a hedge on your left. When you reach a waymark arrow, turn right across the field, heading for the left end of a wood. Continue with the wood on your right, finally entering an enclosed and shady pathway out to a meadow. Walk along this field to cross a stile. Now continue rightish to another two stiles leading to a farm track. (1¹/₂ miles)

④ Turn right to a road. Continue in an easterly direction to **White Cottage**. Turn left at a concrete public footpath sign and follow the field edge, ignoring a path to the left but bearing right (south-east) to reach **Pole Lane**. This leads downhill to the main road. At the T-junction turn right briefly, cross the road and go onto a footpath by a concrete public footpath sign for a few yards. Then turn right at the field corner. Turn left over a plank bridge and walk towards the bridge

over the **River Brain**. Cross this, bearing right uphill to turn right behind the tall row of trees and follow the track all the way to **Fambridge Hall**. Past the Hall, turn right down what is marked 'Private Road' (public footpath) to reach **Station Road**. Turn right over a ford and road bridge across the river to the main road where you will find the **Cross Keys**. (2¹/₂ miles)

⑤ After your lunch break, turn right out of the pub and walk up the main road for a few yards to the church.

*It is worth taking a look round this ancient church. The Norman masons shaped a Saxon headstone into one of their window frames. This window frame is now in the vestry, with a rare glass portrait set in it. The villagers are also proud of two 16th-century roundels in a modern dormer window.*

Leave the churchyard to the south-east, along a hedged lane to the right of the adjoining school. Cross an estate road and soon cross another narrow road. Keep to the right of a hedge ahead on the left and go along the field to an elegant farmhouse called **Whiteways**. Here, turn right at a waymark and walk south-west, soon joining the farm track to the road. Turn left along the road for a few yards and turn right

---

THE CROSS KEYS, NOTLEY

into a concrete yard at **Maltings Farm**. At the back of the yard follow a blue bridleway arrow onto a wide path below the field edges on either side. The lane is quaintly called **Pink Lane**. It runs for about ¹/₂ mile before emerging on a concrete track at the edge of the field. Turn right at a T-junction and go through a metal gate to turn left. Round a few bends, pass **Troys Hall** and reach a country road. Turn right for 200 yards and turn left to **Fairstead church**. (2¹/₂ miles)

*Fairstead church has an Elizabethan shingled spire. There was once a Roman villa nearby and some of the bricks have been incorporated into the church wall halfway along the chancel. Few villages in the county are more remote than Fairstead and even fewer have their very own war grave.*

⑥ Continue your walk on the path to the east of the church, crossing a series of four stiles. You are now climbing on a path left between two fields. At the corner turn right and walk along the side of a wood. After 100 yards spot a gap and turn left into the wood. Go through the wood by a barely visible path; bear slightly right after 30 yards and follow a yellow arrow, pointing left, on a tree branch. Shortly after this, reach the edge of the wood over a bridge and stile. Cross a narrow field and turn right with a hedge on your left. (¹/₂ mile)

⑦ Some 200 yards later, turn left and right to walk uphill at the side of a large field, with the hedge on your left. You will see **Terling windmill** to your right. At the top, turn right and walk downhill all the way to the road as it enters the village. Turn left past some pretty cottages and, just opposite the **Rayleigh Arms** pub, turn right to the village hall and your car. (1 mile)

*Date walk completed:*

# GOSFIELD TO BEAZLEY END

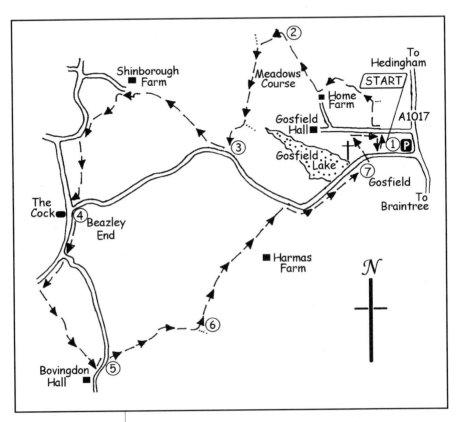

**Distance:**
9³/₄ miles

**Starting point:**
The playing fields car park in Gosfield. GR 781296

**Map: OS Explorer 195 Braintree & Saffron Walden**

**How to get there:** *Gosfield lies between Braintree and Sible Hedingham on the A1017 just under 3 miles north of its junction with the A131. When you reach the centre of Gosfield turn west near the Kings Head public house into Church Road.*

GOSFIELD LAKE IS A HIVE OF ACTIVITY IN THE SUMMER

This walk starts in the centre of Gosfield village and makes its way north via a series of little fenced paths into open countryside round the edge of the old park. The route takes you on some of the old service roads associated with the former Gosfield airfield and then over a pretty golf course. More open fields and bridleways follow as you head north-west and then south to Beazley End. After a stop at the friendly Cock inn, there are more wide views over open fields to enjoy. Another series of tracks and bridleways takes you through the back of nowhere to the road near Gosfield lake where you can call in to the café for an ice cream. The final route back to your car is on a pretty little local path past the church towards historic Gosfield Hall and on to the playing fields.

The **Cock** in Beazley End is a popular establishment with a friendly atmosphere. It is a long narrow building with two main bars, one small bar and a good-sized, lavishly furnished restaurant. The right-hand bar has at the far end a small eating area, equally lavish. Walkers are made to feel very much at home and we enjoyed a delicious Sunday lunch served with a generous helping of vegetables. There is a wide choice of beer and other liquid refreshment. The Cock does tend to get busy at the weekend so it is best to ring to book your table if you are walking on Saturday or Sunday.

**Telephone:** *01371 850566.*

# The Walk

① Cross the playing field, making for a squeeze gap in the fence in the left-hand corner. Turn left for a few feet along the road then right at the next footpath sign. You will find yourself walking a twisting twitten along the backs of the gardens of the houses till you come to a local footpath sign and a wide meadow. Turn left along the left edge of the field out to an old airfield road. Turn left along the road then left again at the next yellow arrow to cross a wide field on a wide track; halfway across a hedge appears on your left. At the road turn right to **Home Farm** and another old road. Walk north-west past the gates with the yellow arrow for about ¹/₂ mile. (1¹/₂ miles)

② When you reach a kissing gate and two yellow arrows, take the left turn into a large field. Keep the hedge and trees on your left to head for the left-hand field corner and a smaller opening out onto the narrow road by a post with a yellow arrow. Turn left and go through the gate. You soon find yourself on a golf course and arrive at a small hut. Keep straight ahead till the track divides. Take the right fork. There is a footpath sign hidden in the hedge on your left. After the metal gate, bear left and make your way out to the road on a farm track. (³/₄ mile)

③ Turn right and walk along the road for 265 yards to the next corner where you will see a cottage on the bend and a bridleway sign. Your route continues ahead down the track. Follow this for ³/₄ mile. When the farm comes into view on your right ignore the track right. Continue ahead for a few more yards till the track you are walking on turns sharp right. You will find a post with a double yellow banding in the hedge on your right; follow this track out to the road near the direction post through **Shinborough Farm**. Continue up this road to a post marked 'footpath number 23'. Turn left here near the overhead lines and keep to the right-hand edge of the field. After 200 yards find a gap on your right and follow this narrow bridleway with a wire fence on your right all the way out to the road. Turn left. Just past a red painted metal gate on your left turn left off the road onto a bridleway heading due south. This bridleway eventually passes a bungalow and probably horses and comes out onto

the road. Turn left and walk a few feet to the **Cock** inn at Beazley End. (2¼ miles)

④ Refreshed, turn right from the pub, then keep right at the junction ¼ mile further on. Now walk for another ¼ mile to arrive at **Great Codham Hall**. Turn left down a gravel track, admiring the views as you go. Under the telephone lines keep right of a farm gate. Your route is now though the woods on your left. However, the footpath was blocked when we walked, so until this is cleared we suggest you make

**THE COCK, BEAZLEY END**

your way carefully round the east side of the wood and cross the ditch. For up to date information on this obstruction ring the Rights of Way Officer of Essex County Council. Walk over the crossing track and take the track south-east. Walk uphill, then as it drops down turn left and right round pheasant shelters and climb the hill, continuing ahead to the trees and under overhead lines. Turn 10 paces left. Cross the stile to go over a short field to a stile opposite and out onto the road. Turn left for 100 yards. (1³/₄ miles)

⑤ On your right you will see a concrete road marked 'Private No Entry' going off to the right; even though the footpath sign is missing this is your onward route. Turn right and walk north-east along this road for just over ¹/₂ mile when you will find a yellow arrow then a concrete footpath sign. Pass two paths coming in from your left and one to your right. Ignore all these and keep ahead till you come to a bridleway sign by a seat carved out of an old tree trunk. This is a lovely quiet place for a picnic. (1 mile)

⑥ Turn left along the farm track heading north-east all the way out to the road, a distance of about 1¹/₄ miles. On your way ignore the footpath left to the livery stables and the track to **Harmas Farm** nestling in the fields down on your

right. As you approach the road you get super long views of **Gosfield Hall** across the valley. Turn right at the road and walk with care about ¹/₂ mile to pass **Gosfield Lake** on your left. Here, on sunny days, you will find waterskiers skimming across the water and campers enjoying this lovely location. Walkers are made welcome at the resort café and you may choose to stop for a well-earned rest, a cup of tea or even an ice cream while you watch the fun. (1³/₄ miles)

*Gosfield Hall was built in warm Tudor brick by Sir John Wentworth during the reign of Henry VII. Originally it had a substantial gatehouse and, to help keep it secure, no windows were provided at ground level. Queen Elizabeth stayed here twice. In the 18th century, Horace Walpole visited the Hall and wrote a mixture of good and bad comments in a letter, including: 'The house is vast, built round a very old court that has never been fine.' He describes Madam's dressing room as 'very pretty and furnished with white damask, china, loads of easy chairs, bad pictures and some pretty enamels'. However, his admiration for the park was wholehearted. One of the many interesting things about the Hall is its wooden donkey gin – the only one in England, we are told – a pre-steam engine for pumping water. Gosfield Park, which was of some 50 acres, included the fine lake and is said to have been one of the best examples of Essex landscape design. The Hall was reconstructed towards the end of the 17th century, and further alterations were carried out in the early Georgian period. The Hall is open from May to September on Wednesday and Thursday afternoons. Telephone: 01787 472914.*

⑦ Retrace your steps to the road and turn left. At the end of the black railings on the right, go up the slope on your right and walk along the left field edge with the road just over the hedge on your left. At the footpath sign, turn left, cross the road and walk past the church to the footpath sign on your left. This well-walked cross-field path takes you through parkland to the railings near Gosfield Hall. Turn right onto

the concrete road and walk back to the familiar gap in the fence on your right, the playing field and your car (³/₄ mile)

*Gosfield church was built in the 1430s, with the chancel and Wentworth Chapel dating from about the same time as the original hall. In the churchyard there is a monument to ten English 'Poor Clares' who in 1795 fled from the terrors of the French Revolution.*

*Date walk completed:*

# GREAT MAPLESTEAD TO AUDLEY END, GESTINGTHORPE

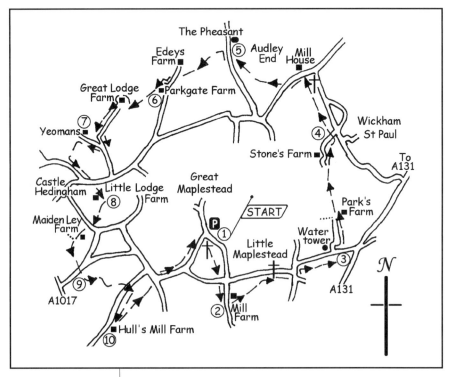

**Distance:**
12¼ miles

**Starting point:**
The small village car
park opposite the
school in Monks
Lodge Road, Great
Maplestead.
GR 808347

**Map:** OS Explorer 195 Braintree & Saffron Walden

**How to get there:** Great Maplestead lies about 3 miles
north of Halstead and halfway between the A131 and the
A1017. From either road follow local signs to Great
Maplestead. When you arrive in the centre of the village you
are heading for the junction of Monks Lodge Road, Lucking
Street and Church Street near the church.

*T*his splendid circuit is in one of the finest walking areas in Essex and has the advantage of being only a short drive from both Braintree and Colchester. The countryside is one of rolling hills and wide open views. The route takes in the delightful churches of Great Maplestead, Little Maplestead and Wickham St Paul and stops for lunch at Audley End in the village of Gestingthorpe, a little way south of Over Hall, the childhood home of the famous explorer Captain Oates. Later you head for the old town of Castle Hedingham, with its Norman keep, and then pass through more hilly country and some beautiful woods to return to Great Maplestead.

The **Pheasant** in Audley End, Gestingthorpe, is a lovely country pub that stands high enough for over twenty Essex churches to be visible from the delightful back garden on a clear day. You will find a fine selection of beers and other drinks and the menu should appeal to all tastes. Bar snacks including baguettes, beefburgers, ploughman's and jacket potatoes are supplemented by two blackboard menus displaying choices of the day. There is also an à la carte menu. This popular place does get busy at weekends, so it is as well to ring ahead and book your table.

**Telephone:** *01787 461196.*

## The Walk

① From the car park, turn left into **Lucking Street**. Just opposite the village hall, turn right up the steps beside the footpath sign to take a well-walked path with a hedge on your right into the churchyard.

*The impressive church in Great Maplestead is set high on a hill and stands on a Norman base. The choir inside is nearly 800 years old and some of the nearby cottages date from the 15th and 16th centuries.*

Bear left to the left-hand corner by the large tree and exit the churchyard through a gap in the hedge to walk downhill across a large field to a yellow arrow. Continue straight on down some steps and walk on with the hedge on your left. Ignore the first yellow arrow and the bridge on your left. Turn right; cross a home-made stile into a meadow beside some tall

**THE CHURCH AT GREAT MAPLESTEAD**

willow trees. Walk with the hedge on your left. Look on your left for a stile, a stout bridge with a handrail and a second stile, by a yellow arrow. Cross over the stream. The next section is extremely pretty. Climb the hill ahead to go under the tall tree beside a wire fence. You will now have 360° views over the surrounding valleys. Walk on to the gate and direction post. Cross the road into **Mill Lane** opposite and continue walking in the same direction till you are just past **Mill Farm** on the bend. (³/₄ mile)

② Follow the footpath sign on your left, heading east. Climb the stile, then walk beside the fence on your left and head for and cross a second stile. There follows a steady uphill climb for approximately 500 yards. You should be on the left of the hedge but if the crops block your way there is normally a good track on the right and you can pop through to the other side just as soon as you are able. At the end of the hedge, turn left to a footpath sign and the road. Turn right and walk past **Maplestead Hall and church**, unless curiosity gets the better of you and you stop to visit this unusual church. You may even wish to take a small rest here in the peace of the countryside. When you reach the T-junction, turn left, then right into **Cock Road**. About ¹/₂ mile further on, reach a water tower. (1¹/₂ miles)

*Little Maplestead church is known as the Little Round Church and is the smallest of four medieval round churches built by the Knights Hospitallers, the others being in London, Cambridge and Northampton. The aisle goes round the entire 30 ft width of the nave. The Hospitallers are said to have worshipped here for 200 years until their preceptory was dissolved under Henry VIII.*

③ Turn left to **Park's Farm**. You soon pass a trig point on your right. When you reach the farm ignore the footpath sign on your left and walk straight ahead into the garden with the vegetable garden on your left (alas, no bridleway sign to help you) and, keeping ahead, walk on along a mown path into an open field. Your route is now right, along the edge of the field, into a section which can be muddy. At the blue arrow, turn right and at the next junction marked by a yellow arrow, turn left onto a long concrete track with the hedge on your right. This track takes you all the way past **Stone's Farm** on your left and down the magnificent wide drive to the road. At the 30 mph sign, turn right along the road. Pass the village green on your right, and you will

spot the **Victory Inn**, Wickham St Paul's busiest watering hole. You may wish to rest here awhile, either to grab a quick pint or have a picnic on the green. (1¹/₂ miles)

*Wickham St Paul was linked for a thousand years to its owner, St Paul's Cathedral in London. The houses surround a large and pleasant green with a pond and a pub. The church stands some ¹/₂ mile to the north, near a farm, and has been in existence since before the other St Paul's was destroyed in the Great Fire!*

④ Now make your way into **Shellards Lane**, passing the duck pond on your right. At the end of the lane, follow the line of the last garden on your right, straight on into a large field on a normally marked path towards and under the power lines. After about ¹/₂ mile, a hedge on your right joins your onward route. This leads to a wooden bridge. Your path is straight on across two more fields, passing the rear of pretty **Wickham St Paul's church** where another hedge appears on your right and marks your route out to the road. Turn left and walk past **Mill House** to the footpath sign at the next bend. Continue to walk over the field in the same direction, heading half right to the far corner and into a dip, where you will find a waymark post with a yellow arrow. Cross into the next field and with the hedge on your left walk uphill through a series of fields. The route on the OS map then shows you going round **Rectory Farm** and into **Audley End**. However, there is no evidence of an exit from the field this way. We followed the footsteps of the locals and continued ahead till we reached the road, then walked right, inside the field edge, to make our way out just before the farm. Turn right and walk up to the **Pheasant** pub. (1½ miles)

⑤ After lunch, cross the road and take the footpath directly opposite the pub. Cross the bridge and walk with the ditch on your right. Turn right and then left round the field edge to a gap in the hedge. Turn half right, then left (do not go through the second gap in the hedge). With the hedge on your right walk round the corner towards a large oak tree. Stay on the field-edge path left, with the hedge on your right for one more field edge. You will see the roof of a building ahead. At the next corner, look for a bridge on your right to take you straight ahead into the next field; walk beside the farm building and out onto the road. Turn left and continue down the road for ¼ mile to **Parkgate Farm** buildings, built in 1899. (1 mile)

THE PHEASANT, AUDLEY END

*Gestingthorpe was the childhood home of a delicate little boy who, as he grew up walked the local lanes and visited Edeys and Parkgate farms. His home was Over Hall, some 1/2 mile north of the Pheasant pub, near the church. Captain Lawrence Edward Oates was involved in an expedition to South Africa where he just missed getting the Victoria Cross. While serving in India with the Inniskilling Dragoons he wrote to Scott and asked if there was a chance he could join his Antartic Expedition – the rest, as they say, is history.*

⑥ At a footpath sign, turn right in front of some outbuildings, onto a grass track. As the track bends right, go straight ahead to cross the field on an unmarked path to a yellow arrow. There is a triangular yellow danger sign on the power cable pole nearby. The waymark post directs you to cross the field and walk with the hedge on your right. Follow a series of yellow arrows right and left around **Great Lodge Farm** till you come to a concrete drive. Turn right and walk down the drive under the power lines and out to another small side road. Turn right and pass beautiful **Keepers Cottage** on your way to **Yeomans** on the right, opposite the footpath sign. (1 1/2 miles)

⑦ Turn left across the stile and

perhaps stop in the lovely green meadow for a picnic or just a rest. **Hedingham Castle** is hidden in the far trees on your left. Walk down the hill to the stile where you should get a glimpse of it. The route into town is along a good urban path. Come out at a road and turn left into **Bayley Street**. Walk past the entrance to the castle or, if you have time, why not stop to visit this well-preserved historical site? Your onward route out of town continues along **Bayley Street**. Turn left into **Sudbury Road**. Ignore the first footpath on your left but look for a sign and steps leading up from the road on your right. Cross, with care, and climb up to the footpath which continues behind the gardens. When you reach the yellow arrow, turn left to cross the open field to the large oak tree and go out to the stile opposite. The farm ahead is **Little Lodge Farm**. (1 mile)

*Castle Hedingham's castle is in fact a mighty Norman keep built in 1140 on the slope of a hill and held by the De Veres for 600 years. This is all that is left of the medieval castle, which was visited over the years by Henry VII, Henry VIII and Queen Elizabeth I. The building is normally open to the public from one week before Easter to the end of October.*

⑧ Do not cross the stile but turn right along the track with the hedge on your left. Turn left, right, left and right again to walk under power lines and out to the road. Cross the road and walk up the drive to pass **Maiden Ley Farm** on your left. Turn left and walk through an area of market gardens, following the many yellow arrows for the **Mills Walk**. You follow first a wire fence on your left, then cross a bridge and eventually walk past another cottage on your way out to the road along the line of the old railway track. (1 mile)

⑨ Turn right and walk downhill. Look out for a mirror and footpath sign on your right to indicate your route left along a narrow road, passing cottages. Turn left up the last field edge, still on the **Mills Walk**, and then right round the field edge. Through a gate you come to an area where you might find some ducks. Following the yellow arrows on a good path, you enter a beautiful wood and climb through it onto a quiet road. Turn right downhill. In a few yards, on your right, you will see an opening in the hedge. Go through this, crossing a stile, and use the permissive path to enjoy magnificent views as you descend to the valley bottom. Go over another stile and back out onto the road. (1 mile)

⑩ When you come to the wonderful mill buildings, look out for **Hulls Mill Farm**. Turn left up the short gravel runway and head for the red-brick wall gap and wooden fencing to the left of the garden. Once you get there you will find a family of yellow signs to assist you. Make your way out into the farmyard and head uphill, north-east, over a series of stiles. Continue uphill, stopping occasionally to look back at the fine views. Walk with the barbed wire fence on your left till you come into a large field. Turn half right and walk with the hedge on your left, gently uphill to the footpath sign and the road. Take the road directly opposite that leads into **Great Maplestead**. You can relax now – the last mile is along this road. It descends as it passes **Barretts Hall**. Keep left at the fork and climb uphill again into **Great Maplestead**. Pass the entrance to the church and then cross half left into the car park for the end of the walk and a well-earned rest (1½ miles)

*Date walk completed:*

# HOCKLEY WOODS TO HULLBRIDGE

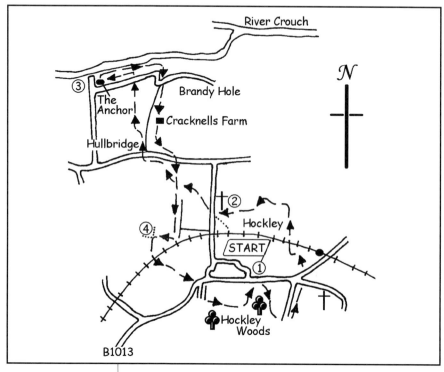

| **Distance:** | **Map: OS Explorer 175 Southend-on-Sea & Basildon** |
|---|---|
| 8 miles | |

**Starting point:**
The parking area at Great Bull Wood, Hockley Woods.
GR 833923

**How to get there:** *From the west and north of the county travel south from Rettendon turnpike on the A130. At Rawreth turn left at the traffic lights and follow the signs to Rochford. In Hockley keep an eye out for the Bull pub and just past this turn right into the narrow entrance marked Hockley Woods. From Southend travel either by Rayleigh or Rochford via the B1013 to reach the woods either just after the Bull or just before it.*

THE 12TH CENTURY CHURCH OF ST PETER AND ST PAUL, HOCKLEY

*H*ockley is situated on a ridge between the rivers Crouch and Thames. This route invites you to park in Hockley Woods, to walk along a section of the Boundary Walk round these woods and then to make your way north through part of Hockley parish to the summit of Plumberow Mount, a Roman mound whose original purpose is unknown. Here you can pause to take in the marvellous views over the Crouch valley and beyond to the south of the Dengie peninsula. The walk continues through beautiful woodland with frequent spectacular panoramas, and then on to the riverside Anchor inn in Hullbridge. After lunch you soon strike back inland and follow the edge of Blounts Wood to return to Hockley Woods and your car.

84

The **Anchor** in Hullbridge is a vibrant pub. It has a surprisingly big bar with an even bigger garden fronting onto the riverside. The yacht clubs opposite and adjacent to the pub mean that there is plenty of activity on the river. Children will love the play areas available at this family orientated hostelry. There is a wide range of food – cooked meals, sandwiches and burgers – with plenty of beers, lagers and ciders to wash it down.

**Telephone:** *01702 230205.*

 *The Walk*

① Having parked in **Hockley Woods** locate on the east side of the parking area a large wooden sign marked '**Boundary Walk**'. Behind that is a yellow arrow and a small gate. Go through this and walk on a visible path that runs near the edge of the woods. After 300 yards the path bears right and you come to a blue sign of the **Roach Valley Way**. Here you turn left over two bridges and follow a narrow twitten out to **Woodland Road**. Turn left to reach the main street in **Hockley**. Cross this at a zebra crossing and turn right down **Spa Road**. Now be careful – just after a shop named First Choice, turn left and at a concrete public footpath signpost enter a narrow twitten leading to a white kissing gate and a level railway crossing. Cross with care and keep on the main path in **Marylands Wood** near the back of gardens belonging to houses on the right.

*These are ancient woods and are being restored with the help of the British Trust for Conservation Volunteers.*

A few hundred yards after leaving the woods a path turns to the left on **Plumberow Mount**.

*This is believed to be of Roman origin. Although excavated in the last century, its purpose is still a mystery. There are some magnificent views and on a fine day Danbury church near Chelmsford can be seen to the north-west.*

Follow this path to the west, and cross a field boundary by a plank bridge. Turn right and then left at the field corner. Enter **Crabtree Wood** by a stile and soon cross a plank bridge.

*The woods hereabouts have a long history and the manmade banks that criss-cross them were built to mark ownership.*

Later the path widens into a track. When the track turns sharply to the left, find a concrete public footpath post and continue in the same direction along a narrow path.

*A magnificent oak tree is near the fence on your left. It is believed to be at least 250 years old. Behind this is Hockley Hall. This is the site of the original manor of Hockley and is mentioned in the Domesday Book. The thatched building is the old school house, built in 1841 at a cost of £540. There was a windmill to the rear of Mill House until the 19th century.*

Turn right at a public footpath sign down into the churchyard of **Hockley church**. (2 miles)

*The church of St Peter and St Paul dates from the 12th century but it was King Canute who first planted a church on this hilltop.*

② Turn left in front of the church onto the road and turn right for a few yards to the entrance to **Wadham Park Farm**.

*Wadham Park Farm gets its name from Wadham College, Oxford, which once owned all the land in the area and to this day is responsible for the living of Hockley church.*

Here you will see a public footpath post pointing diagonally across the fields to **Hullbridge**. Follow this diagonally left. After 100 yards cross a stile, then spy and cross two further stiles. Aim for the fence at the bottom of the field and turn left along it to the field corner where you cross another stile. Now walk between a hedge and a fence to a stile and plank bridge onto a hedged track (**Blounts Wood Lane**). Turn right to reach **Lower Road**, where you turn left. Ignore two footpath signs on the right and turn right at the third sign into **Long Lane**. Pass some houses and continue on a broad farm track. Soon you will reach a path crossing and should turn left off **Long Lane**.

*Long Lane derives its name from Ernest Long who served on the parish council from 1964 to 1978.*

This path leads round a field, following a rail fence, and to the left over a substantial pedestrian bridge. Turn right along an estate road till you reach **Keswick Avenue**. Turn right and soon left at a public footpath sign. Along this path you come to a residential park which you walk through to the river. Turn left for 400 yards to the **Anchor** pub for a deserved break. (2 miles)

*For many years there has been an inn on this riverside site, just at the point where it was most practical to ford the Crouch. In the days when South Woodham Ferrers was little more than a few houses around the railway halt, regular traffic made its way from there to Hullbridge. A friend's mother living in South Woodham Ferrers used to go to school each day in Hullbridge. As the river is a few feet deep even at low tide, how was this done? The answer is by horse and cart! Pilgrims crossed the river here on their way to Canterbury, offering up prayers at the now demolished chapel of St Thomas à Becket. Near the*

*pub the attractive Anchor Cottages are said to be at least 400 years old.*

③ After your lunch break retrace your steps to the park. Walk diagonally left across the park to a side road. Turn left and then right at a corner. At the next corner leave the road to join **Long Lane** running south. Follow this lane through **Cracknell's Farm**. Some 300 yards beyond the farm buildings turn left off the lane at a footpath crossways and walk along this path diagonally, then turn right to **Lower Road**. Here turn left past a footpath sign

THE ANCHOR, HULLBRIDGE

to turn right at the second footpath sign up **Blounts Wood Lane**.

*Blounts Wood Lane is an ancient greenway that leads to the early medieval manor of Blounts Farm, now the other side of the railway. The parish boundary between Hullbridge and Hockley runs down the centre of the lane.*

Keep along this well-defined track for ³/₄ mile. As you approach the railway line turn right onto a grass track and walk past the northern edge of **Blounts Wood**. (2¹/₂ miles)

④ At the end of the wood turn left onto a path in the wood and follow the path south for 300 yards. As the path begins to turn right you turn left (east) for a few yards and cross a pedestrian railway bridge. Continue east on a well-marked path climbing towards a farm. Look out for a sign where the path changes over from the right to the left of the fence and keep on this side to pass a house on the left and farm buildings on the right (**Home Farm**), out to the B1013. Cross this busy road with care and walk a few yards to the left, where you will see metal railings on your right giving access to **Woodside Road** behind the houses on the main road. Walk down **Woodside Road**, turning left at the end. At the end of the road walk straight on into an earth path running east. Join a crossing shale path and turn right to cross a bridge. Turn left and get to a wide forest path. Follow the signs, walking north-east, and soon reach the parking area at **Great Bull Wood**, where you will find your car. (1¹/₂ miles)

 *Date walk completed:*

# MUNDON TO
# COLD NORTON

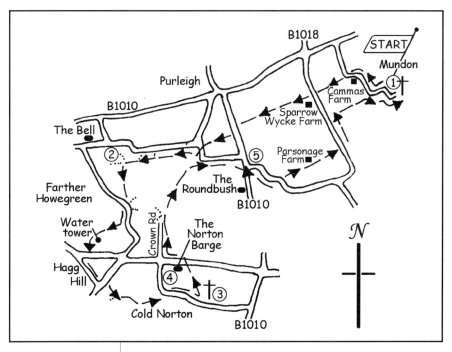

**Distance:**
9³/₄ miles

**Starting point:**
Near the church in
Mundon.
GR 879026

Maps: OS Explorer 176 Blackwater Estuary, with a very small
section on 183 Chelmsford & The Rodings

**How to get there:** *Travelling on the B1010 from the A414
east of Danbury, pass Purleigh to reach the T-junction with
Fambridge Road. Turn right and immediately left along Blind
Lane, go over the crossroads into New Hall Lane and after
200 yards turn right up Vicarage Lane. This little road has no
diversion and you go past Mundon Hall to come to
Mundon church hiding behind the trees to the right of a
pond. You can park near the church, but take care not to
block access to a field.*

*T*his is an excellent walk starting from the remote redundant church at Mundon and continuing to Purleigh Hill, close to the possible site of a Norman castle. The first part of the route from Mundon to Purleigh mainly follows the St Peter's Way, a 45 mile long distance route from Chipping Ongar to St Peter's on the Wall. We then head to Farther Howegreen and round the golf course to Norton Hall and church with its spectacular view to the Blackwater Estuary. After lunch at the Norton Barge pub in Cold Norton we head back to Mundon by way of field paths and quiet roads, having crossed a dismantled railway line no less than four times.

The friendly **Norton Barge** at Cold Norton is a freehouse adjacent to the old railway line. Over the years it has been called the Railway Tavern, Barnside Tavern, the Norton, and then the Norton Barge. It seems that the owner of the Barge at the time of the final name change had once been a lighterman on the Thames and to this day there are in the building oars and other bric-a-brac connected to the waterside. Opposite the pub are former railway houses, and the station in Cold Norton was nearby. A fine restaurant is open in the evening, and at lunchtime the bar menu is varied and good value with many main course dishes and also jacket potatoes, sandwiches, and baguettes. The beers available are Bass, Greene King IPA and Crouch Vale Essex Gold.

**Telephone:** *01621 829569.*

 *The Walk*

*Mundon seems lonely in its situation, though recently the paths from here to Maylandsea and Latchingdon have been reorganised for easier following and also so that the farmer can maintain them with ease. Such is the diligence of the Ramblers'*

*Association. It is worth entering the little church in Mundon to catch the atmosphere of bygone days. Round the hall and the church there are extensive traces of a moat which when complete in Norman times must have been effective.*

① From the church walk back along **Vicarage Lane**. Turn right at a corner where an old cottage has

**THE ROUTE PASSES BY THIS HUGE WATER TOWER**

been extensively refurbished. Past **Cammas Farm** you come to a five-barred gate on the left with a stile alongside. Cross this to the right and walk with a hedge on your right for 300 yards, crossing two more stiles on the way to the road. Cross this road slightly to the left and enter the drive to **Sparrow Wycke Farm**. Just opposite the rather ornate farm house turn right through a gateway and walk downhill in a rough pasture to a stile in the middle of the facing hedge. Having crossed this, make for the far left corner in the next field and a plank bridge

with two stiles. Turn right along the next field to cross another plank bridge and continue to a hedge where your walk line follows the hedge on your right. Reach a gate with an improvised stile fixed on to reach the road. Turn left for a few yards to cross a stile on the right, with a hedge on your left. Over another plank bridge come to a projecting hedge which you follow with the hedge on the left to a gap at the end. Go through this and continue for a few yards to cross a gate on the right onto a lane. Turn left along this lane. Shortly a footpath sign points back to the right and the path follows diagonally across this little field to the corner. Now turn left and walk by the visible path to reach the mound of the dismantled railway. Steps have been installed on both sides of the mound to help your progress and, having negotiated these, walk on to reach a field at the base of **Purleigh Hill**. Cross a stile and walk up the hill, with the hedge on your left, to the top corner, crossing another stile on the way. (3 miles)

*The railway once ran from Witham to South Woodham Ferrers. There were two stations in Maldon. The west station connected to a halt near Purleigh, then Cold Norton, later linking with the Southend–Wickford route to London. The line was closed in 1939, though during the war it was used for the transport of munitions.*

② Here you should turn left over two rather awkward stiles. From the point before you cross the double stiles, 200 yards to your right you can find the **Bell** where food and drink are available. The views are spectacular back down the hill.

*Purleigh is a special village in Essex. No less a person than the great-great-grandfather of George Washington was rector here in 1633. The Royalist sympathies of Lawrence Washington caused his ejection from the living in 1643. Later he was curate at Little Braxted and was eventually buried in All Saints' church at Maldon. His son emigrated to America and so emerged the dynasty which had such an important part to play in the founding of America. In those days Purleigh was contained on the top of Church Hill – the church, the pub, the hall and all the houses. It is also conjectured that 200 yards south was the site of a castle but reliable proof of this has yet to be established.*

The route continues downhill across the field to a gap in the facing hedge and along a green lane for barely 100 yards. This short distance can be quite overgrown in summer and a trifle muddy in winter. When you reach **Farther Howegreen** turn left and then right along a defined path uphill to the road. Turn left along the road for a few yards. When the road turns left, turn right uphill on a field edge. Keep on this track round a corner till you reach a path to the left, normally reinstated diagonally across the large field towards the huge water tower. Walk round the tower and take the field edge south to the road by a gap and public footpath post. Turn right along the road and at the corner turn left down **Hagg Hill**. This is one-way coming towards you so there should be no traffic coming from behind. At the bottom turn left. Just past a bus stop you will see a footpath post. Turn right by a stile onto a golf course and cross two further stiles and a pedestrian bridge. Unlike many golf courses there are very few indicators of the walking route through. Having crossed the bridge, walk on over rough ground between a teeing area and a hedge to a yellow-topped water sign. Now turn leftish across a fairway and join a straight grass track with a hedge on your left and a succession of water signs. Continue on this track (**Wrights Lane**) to a rusty old metal gate leading out of the golf course onto a road. Turn right and walk uphill for 400 yards to the pretty church by **Norton Hall**. This would be a wonderful picnic site. The views of the **Blackwater Estuary** to the north-east are something special. (2³/₄ miles)

③ From the church join the path meandering north-west downhill to the woods and keep to this path close to the dismantled railway to reach the **Cold Norton** road. Turn left over the one-way bridge with

THE NORTON BARGE, COLD NORTON

traffic lights and soon come to the **Norton Barge** pub for your lunch break. ($^1/_2$ mile)

④ After lunch continue up the road and turn right into **Crown Road**. This becomes a footpath. Cross a stile and turn left along a grass path for 15 yards. Turn right into a thicket, passing two houses with large areas of garden. Cross another stile into a pasture field and follow the hedge on the right down to a stile in the facing hedge that leads you into a byway. Turn right and stay with this to the point where you go through the remains of a railway bridge. Bear slightly right and soon you will come to the corner of **Roundbush Road**. Walk up this (having kept to the right) and after passing two smart houses

you reach the **Roundbush pub**. ($1^1/_2$ miles)

⑤ Turn right along a layby to the end. Turn left and cross the main road into **Burnham Road**. This road takes you past **Roundbush Farm** and later you turn left at a footpath post to pass **Parsonage Farm** and **Mundon Furze** to the road. Turn left and nearly opposite the village hall turn right at a footpath post on a track through the fields to two houses. Now you can retrace your steps to **Mundon Hall** and church, where you left your car. (2 miles)

*Date walk completed:*

94

# HEYBRIDGE BASIN TO GOLDHANGER

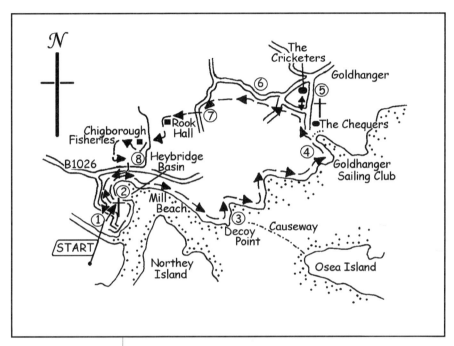

**Distance:**
8¹⁄₂ miles

**Starting point:**
Daisy Lane car park
(free) at Heybridge
Basin.
GR 871068

**Map: OS Explorer 176 Blackwater Estuary**

**How to get there:** *From Chelmsford take the A414 through Danbury, and the northern Maldon bypass leads to the causeway at Heybridge. From here follow the Goldhanger signs and turn right, where signposted, to Heybridge Basin.*

*T*he atmospheric Heybridge Basin is a favourite haunt of walkers, where they can wander by the water and watch the world go by. This route starting from the Basin, with its colourful sailing boats, visits the quaint little parish church before heading out to the sea wall and round to Mill Beach. The views of the Blackwater Estuary are immense. At Decoy Point there is the causeway built by the Romans, which links the mainland with Osea Island at low tide. After a pleasant lunch in the ancient village of Goldhanger, head for home over the fields, passing the Chigborough lakes, to reach the sea wall yet again and finish with a saunter back to the Basin.

The **Cricketers** in Goldhanger is an excellent little pub. The back bar has an old flagged floor whilst the front bar, where much of the eating is done, has smart wooden flooring and shows a neat face to the world. As it is a freehouse there is always a good selection of real ales available. The food menu is varied and has a range of tempting cooked dishes to suit everyone.

**Telephone:** *01621 788250.*

 *The Walk*

*The Chelmer & Blackwater Navigation was opened in the 1790s. The newly built canal made use of the River Chelmer running from Chelmsford, through Maldon and on to Heybridge, then joining the River Blackwater for a time before completing the last mile and a half to Heybridge Basin, which barely existed in pre-canal days.*

① From the car park, walk back to the entrance and follow the village street, north, to the bus stop on the corner. Pass tiny **St George's church** and leave the road at a concrete public footpath post. With the construction of some new houses, the first part of the path has become a twitten between an established garden and some new fencing. Follow the waymarks over a bridge and turn right below the sea wall to the access point leading up to the wall. (¹/₂ mile)

② Now you can enjoy the glorious views over the **Blackwater Estuary.**

THE CREEK NEAR GOLDHANGER

*Close to the shore is Northey Island. Osea Island, nearer the sea coast, and even the towers of Bradwell power station merge into the scenery at this distance. If it is a clear day, you may be able to pick out, just to the right of the power station, the tiny silhouette of St Peter's chapel, built in the 7th century by St Cedd.*

The surface of the path is quite good here and when you reach the two little shops and cafés catering for the large caravan sites around **Mill Beach**, you can make steady progress along a concrete path to

**Decoy Point**. (1 ¹/₂ miles)

*At Decoy Point you reach the causeway where vehicles can drive over to Osea Island around low tide. At the turn of the century, Osea was a home for reforming alcoholics, though sometimes not so reforming, as it is said that Goldhanger residents were bribed to leave bottles tied to rocks on the island shores to be recovered at lower tides. Please note that there are no public rights of way on the island and public access is only available with the permission of the owner.*

97

③ Turn left along the sea wall, briefly heading north. All at once the nature of the countryside becomes wilder, the seabirds' cries are more dominant and in the middle distance is the tower of **Goldhanger church**. Follow the sea wall east. Sometimes the church is lost behind trees but, as you get closer to the village, its size and beauty is overwhelming. (1½ miles)

④ The path turns left past **Goldhanger Sailing Club** and leaves the sea path to turn left for 200 yards along a hedged track by a playing field to the village road. Turn right up this road – later you will find that it is called **Fish Street** which explains why some of the houses have little fishes on their walls and number plates. Walk on past the ancient **Chequers** inn and the church to reach the highly recommended **Cricketers** pub. Now it is time for a drink and something to eat – either a snack or, perhaps, a more substantial cooked meal. (1 mile)

*After lunch, why not linger awhile at the church in Goldhanger? The tower, the chapel, and the three-bay roof of the nave all date from medieval times. The large churchyard, with its many chestnut trees, is a glowing mass of red and gold in autumn.*

⑤ From the pub, retrace your steps

THE CRICKETERS, GOLDHANGER

98

down to the church and turn right up **Head Street**. Perhaps pause to look at the village water pump. This still works and, if you persevere, a substantial flow of water can be produced. Carrying on up **Head Street** you reach the main road. Cross with care to a concrete public footpath sign and follow this path on the field edge behind gardens to a lane. (1 mile)

⑥ Turn left for a few yards to another footpath sign and cross a wide open field due west, navigating carefully for 500 yards to a gap in the hedge ahead to cross a plank bridge over a ditch. Continue for 50 yards to reach a lane and turn left down this, following right and left bends. (1 mile)

⑦ Turn right at a footpath sign along a broad grass path with a hedge on your right. At the end of a field, walk into the farmstead by **Rook Hall** and turn left with a waymark and then right along a farm track to a road. Turn left and soon come to **Chigborough Fisheries**. (¹/₂ mile)

⑧ At a concrete public footpath signpost turn right past a SAGA sign and make your way round the right side of a large fishing lake. After a left turn, go right for 30 yards and follow a waymark left along a wide grass track, passing another lake on the right. Keep on this path to reach the Goldhanger to Maldon road. Just to the left is **Wharf Road**, marked private and leading after 50 yards to the sea wall. This road is often used by locals for access but to gain the right of way it is necessary to walk left along the main road for 100 yards to the **River Mill** pub. Now walk to the left of the pub and join the sea wall through a wooden gate. Turn right along the wall and retrace your route to a large pond fed from the estuary. Turn left and pass the newly reconstructed **Blackwater Sailing Club** building. As is often the case these days, what were once ruined buildings on the site of the mill have been reborn as smart residences. Walk south to **Heybridge Basin**. Reach the **Withey** café on your left and, nearly opposite the **Jolly Sailor** pub on your right, pass the canal lock giving access between the **Blackwater River** and the canal; walk about 50 yards past the **Old Ship** pub to the **Daisy Lane car park**. (2 miles)

*Date walk completed:*

# CANEWDON TO
# PAGLESHAM EAST END

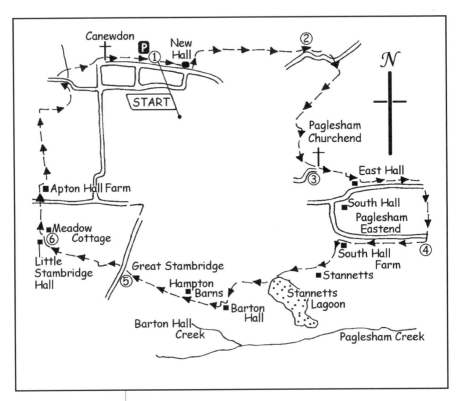

**Distance:**
11½ miles

**Starting point:**
The village hall car
park in Canewdon.
GR 903945

**Map: OS Explorer 176 Blackwater Estuary**

**How to get there:** *Canewdon lies south of the River Crouch,
north-east of Hawkwell which is on the B1013. Make your
way to Ashingdon and then follow signs to Canewdon. When
you get to the Anchor pub, continue round the right-hand
bend, past the village stores. The village hall is on the left, at
the very edge of the village.*

THE PUNCH BOWL AND A ROW OF COTTAGES AT PAGLESHAM CHURCH END

*T*his circuit in the south-east of the county starts from the quaint hilltop village of Canewdon. There are superb views out across Lion Creek and the River Crouch to Althorne and Burnham. Wide open fields bring you to a nature reserve on the edge of the creek, brimming with wildlife. Then it is on to Paglesham, once a well-known haunt of smugglers, and time for lunch at the renowned Plough and Sail. Your return route follows some surprisingly well maintained paths and tracks to take you past a wonderful lagoon and more views over the creeks that are such a feature of this peaceful corner of Essex.

The **Plough and Sail** at Paglesham East End is an ancient, white weatherboard pub. It is popular with walking groups and locals from the Southend area because of its excellent location and good food. A wide range of bar snacks is available, including salads, ploughman's, soup and sandwiches. However, you may be tempted by something more substantial, like the Barnsley lamb chop, shepherd's pie or one of the excellent fish dishes. They serve the thinnest of fish batter here. All the food is cooked to order so don't expect it to arrive in an instant. At busy times, it is advisable to book.

**Telephone:** *01702 258242.*

 *The Walk*

Canewdon, it is said, gets its name from the fact that King Canute fought and won a famous battle hereabouts. He encamped his army near Canewdon before his last great fight with Edmund Ironside.

① From the car park turn left and walk east along the village road past **New Hall**. Just after **Gardeners Lane** look for a footpath sign on your left beside a metal gate. This leads up the track past a yellow arrow to a further gate. Climb the stile on your right and walk down beside the hedge of an open field. When the hedge runs out, go half left on a cross-field path to a yellow arrow, then half left again over a huge field to a bridge. Go half left again to a second bridge, then straight on over another field to some undergrowth.

*All the time you have been in these fields you will have had super views north over the River Crouch to the Dengie peninsula.*

Turn right and walk up the side of the undergrowth. A yellow arrow points you round the left of a pond towards the end of a well maintained garden. Make your way to the road and climb the stile. Immediately look for the entrance to the **Essex Wildlife Trust Lion Creek Nature Reserve**. Enter the reserve and walk with the hedge on your right until, on your right, you find the exit back onto the road. (1¼ miles)

*In late summer, Lion Creek is awash with plants like sea lavender, golden samphire and sea spurrey. The reserve only covers 12 acres but attracts such insects as the Essex skipper and brown argus butterflies, not forgetting the short-winged conehead bush-cricket. Wading birds also visit during the season and short-eared owls hunt here in winter. The entrance to Lower Raypits Reserve, a notable feeding and roosting area for wildfowl and waders, is via this reserve.*

② Turn left and then right on the road passing the end of **Lion Creek** till you come to a footpath sign on your right. Cross the plank bridge and walk on top of the dyke edge. Turn right at the yellow arrow and then cross the open field on a path under overhead lines. When the lines turn right, keep straight on across the field till you reach a wooden fence. Turn left on the sea wall towards **Paglesham Church End church**. Go through the kissing gate and turn right down the slope to an arrow and a grass track by the backwater. The track becomes a concrete path as it leads out to the road. (1¹⁄₂ miles)

*There is only one road into and out of the small hamlet of Paglesham Church End. At the end of the road is the church which is said to have Roman bricks built into its Norman walls. The tower is 16th-century. You will be following in the steps of many a pilgrim before you as you make your way past the 17th-century inn and its neighbouring ancient cottages.*

③ Turn left and walk past the **Punch Bowl** pub, the cottages and church. At **Church Hall Farm**, follow the direction post with the **Roach Valley Way** sign to the left of the garden of **Winton How**. The next yellow arrow directs you along the footpath, first beside the paddock, then out across the field. When you come to a track turn right and then left. You must keep to the field side of **East Hall** farm buildings and there are lots of yellow arrows and footpath signs to assist you. You are directed to a narrow tarmac road, where you turn left and walk east for about ¹⁄₂ mile till you come to a white weatherboard cottage. The footpath you seek is through a small white gate to the left of the house. Walk up the left of the garden to another white gate. Continue with a brick wall on your right out to a field. Walk up the right-hand side of the field to another garden gate, a garden, and a further gate. This brings you into a gravel lane. Carry on in the same direction till you reach the **Plough and Sail** pub and your well-earned rest. (1³⁄₄ miles)

④ After lunch, walk past the lane on which you arrived at the pub, and head west for ¹⁄₂ mile to **South Hall Farm**. To avoid the dangerous bend, join the footpath by walking past **South Hall Farm Cottages**. When you reach the buildings of the farm, turn left, then right, to pick up a waymarked gravel track that goes west, south, and then west again to pass the isolated **Stannetts**. Continue ahead at the gate along the track, following the waymarks. When the track peters out, make your way, first with the hedge on your right, then over open ground, towards a ruined gate and a waymark. A beautiful lake now comes into view. **Stannetts Creek** was dammed to make this perfect lagoon and there is always a lovely variety of birds to see. You may like to sit and watch awhile or even have a picnic here. Suitably refreshed, follow the yellow arrows away from the lake to the right-hand side of a tempting track. The **Roach Valley Way** signs guide you over three field edges and along a hedged path. You then join the tempting track, walking west. Turn

left downhill towards **Barton Hall**, enjoying the views over **Barton Hall Creek** and **Paglesham Reach** as you go. Walk under the power lines, turning left at the next corner, and take the permissive road west, past **Barton Hall**. Along the road, eventually you reach a footpath sign confirming your route through the centre of **Hampton Barns** steading. Later, the paths divide. Take the right-hand track, usually covered in cockleshells, to walk with the hedge on your right and a paddock on your left. In a few steps, come to an open field and walk beneath the power line out to the road at **Great Stambridge**. (3$\frac{1}{2}$ miles)

⑤ Turn right and walk past the **Royal Oak** pub. Turn left up

**THE PLOUGH & SAIL, PAGLESHAM EAST END**

Steward Elm farm lane. When you come to the yellow arrow, bear left and right, cross the stream and take an almost 'royal' route up between the paddocks. At the end of the paddocks, cross an earth bridge, following the arrow right onto a track that turns left. At the next corner, ignore the footpath straight ahead and turn the corner, keeping the ditch on your right. Keep straight on towards the farm buildings of **Little Stambridge Hall** till you reach a point where the track turns sharp left near some paddocks. Just ahead you will find a stile which, alas, did not have an arrow marker when we walked the route. This leads you diagonally over four more stiles and out to a concrete road. (³/₄ mile)

⑥ Turn right on this concrete road and walk past pretty **Meadow Cottage** and straight on over a cross-field path, under power lines, over a bridge, and through an orchard to a stile. Climb the stile to the road. Cross this and continue walking in the same direction up a green track past some old farm buildings to a crossing farm track. At the yellow arrow, turn right to **Apton Hall Farm**. When you are level with the end of the last chicken shed, turn left on a firm track. This leads you north for over ¹/₂ mile, passing a yellow arrow. Walk across an open field to an arrow indicating that the onward route is to the right. Carry on to another track with the hedge on your left. Go left over the earth bridge and round the field edge corner. You are now heading north out to the corner of the road near a footpath sign. Turn left, watching out for the traffic which rushes round the bends on this road. Continue north for a few yards and then go left round the next corner, passing the end of a lane marked 'No right of way'. In another few yards, you will find a footpath sign in the right-hand hedge. Cross the bridge and stile, heading steeply uphill half right to a stile. Climb this and cross the road you previously passed the end of, and make your way over the open field (your last on this walk) to **Canewdon church**. Go through the church gate, which we believe is locked every evening, and head straight on across the churchyard, passing to the right of the church. As you leave the churchyard, you may wish to stop and investigate the old lock-up and stocks. Walk up the road ahead, passing both the **Chequers** and the **Anchor** pubs, to return to the village hall and your car. (2³/₄ miles)

*Date walk completed:*

# FRIDAY WOOD TO FINGRINGHOE

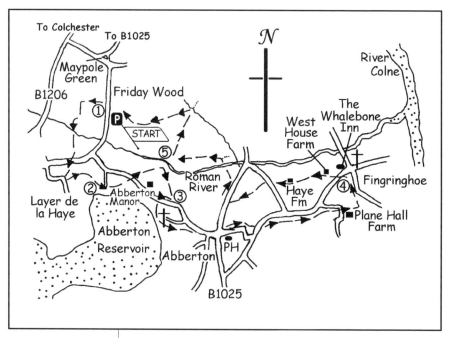

**Distance:**
9¹/₂ miles

Map: OS Explorer 184 Colchester

**Starting point:**
In the large car park
near Fridaywood
Farm.
GR 986209

**How to get there:** *Take the B1026 from the centre of
Colchester and follow Butt Road and Layer Road to turn left
along Berechurch Hall Road. Pass the Maypole pub and turn
right down Bounstead Road. Beyond Fridaywood Farm you
come to a car park on the left.*

THE OLD ANVIL

*T*his walk is full of variety, with woods, rivers and picturesque valleys. From the car park you first cross west and walk over open fields downhill to go through mill buildings alongside the Roman River and on to Abberton Reservoir at Layer de la Haye. There are fine views of the reservoir and, after passing through the village of Abberton, you head on to Fingringhoe, where you can see the oldest oak tree in Essex. The Whalebone pub and lunch await you here, then a village path leads to a super byway to take you further up the valley before you walk down into Man Wood and back to the river. Once over the river, the route takes you through the woods back to your starting point.

The **Whalebone Inn** in Fingringhoe was built 250 years ago. Among the events it has witnessed is a great feast held to celebrate the defeat of Napoleon. Today, the Whalebone is popular for eating as much as drinking, and the options for both are mouthwatering. This is a friendly place, with a well-stocked bar. On a fine day, it is a delight to sit in the large rear garden and take in the fine views of the river valley. An old barn in the grounds is sometimes used to serve refreshments to large groups of ramblers.

▌ **Telephone:** *01206 729307.*

 *The Walk*

*Note: The land which embraces the start and finish of this walk is, in fact, owned by the military. However, the route is wholly on public rights of way. Occasionally, soldiers carry out exercises on this land and will request the cooperation of walkers to divert their route.*

① Leaving the car park at the northern end, go back onto the road you have just driven along. On the other side of this road there is a concrete public footpath sign and you follow this into a field along a track to the west. At the end of the field there are two metal footpath signs. Follow the one to **Malting Green** and soon come to a gate and stile onto a tack leading to the mill. A public footpath sign now says 'Mill Lane'. Pass through the mill buildings and, having descended almost to river level, you now climb

to the **Abberton road**. Turn right and at a house named **Sandland** cross the road and at a footpath sign enter a twitten between two gardens. Now pass a field. The path turns right to a little road and you will see just down this road a footpath sign leading left back into the field. It is usually best to turn right on this field down to the field edge and then walk left along its length to reach the bottom of a broad track. (1¹/₂ miles)

② Cross this track and continue between a fence on your right and a hedge on your left. Walk on in this controlled fashion for 450 yards to the **Abberton road**, crossing two stiles on the way. Go over the road and walk with the hedge on your left for 600 yards to reach a large wooden bridge on your left. To your right you will see a stile and earth bridge over a watercourse. Cross this and walk south, heading for a stile to the left of and below **Abberton Manor**. Now cross the stile and climb through the trees for 250 yards to gain the **Abberton road** again. (1 mile)

③ Turn right briefly and then turn left at a footpath sign, walking towards **Abberton church**. Follow the fence on your right, slightly below the field. As the fence turns to the right, head left uphill across the field to the church gate. Stop here to admire the view all around including the vast reservoir. Walk round to the front of the church and exit by an iron gate to **Rectory Lane**. This leads back to the

**Abberton road**. Turn right and walk up to the village. At the crossroads go over **Mersea Road** and continue on the road to **Fingringhoe**. As the road turns right, join a footpath for 420 yards to rejoin the road. Continue along the road and when it turns left ignore a footpath sign on the right but later turn right along a lane to **Plane Hall Farm**. Turn left before the farm buildings, along a wide track. Some 300 yards later, at the end of a large field, meet a crossing bridleway and turn left, heading north with a glimpse of

THE WHALEBONE INN, FINGRINGHOE

**Fingringhoe church** in the distance. Follow this straight path, later walking along the edge of the village playing field. The path comes onto a road where you turn right, and soon you reach the **Whalebone** public house in Fingringhoe for a welcome break in the middle of your walk. (3 miles)

*Fingringhoe, Rowhedge and Wivenhoe are the three villages grouped around the junction of the River Colne and the Roman River. This latter river was more substantial in prehistoric times and played an important part in determining the boundaries of the tribal capital at Camulodunum. Today, from Great Tey, it flows by Copford and the zoo, then north of Abberton Reservoir to Fingringhoe and the Colne. The place where the Roman River and the Colne join has been painted and photographed countless times and, without doubt, makes a beautiful scene. Fingringhoe roughly translates as 'the spur of the dwellers on the finger', meaning the broad finger of land between the Roman River and Geedon Creek. In 1884 the area was damaged by the great Essex earthquake which resulted in the discovery of two medieval wall paintings in the church. Not far from the village is the Fingringhoe Nature Reserve which is a must for birdwatchers. In the centre of*

*Fingringhoe, next to the village green and pond, stands the oldest oak tree in the county. The story goes that this huge tree grew from an acorn planted in the mouth of an executed pirate over 600 years ago. Another local story is told of how, in the 13th century, King Edward I was at Fingringhoe for a deer hunt. When he recognised one of his washerwomen, Matilda, amongst the followers, he teased her, betting against her joining the hunt on horseback and being in at the kill. She took up the challenge, and stayed the course; the king had to fork out forty shillings. Matilda was a true forerunner of Essex woman!*

④ After your visit to the **Whalebone Inn** set off to the right as you leave the pub car park. Just beyond the village hall, across the street, there is a useful parallel path on the other side of the hedge which makes for a safer journey alongside the road for 350 yards up to **Westhouse Farm**. Here, leave the track and cross the road to the colourful village sign. Take a diagonal route past the farm buildings and walk along this glorious farm track between fields, with the **Roman River** and valley way down to your right. Follow this track for a mile, passing **Haye Farm**, to reach a minor road. Turn right, then immediately go left up a rather rougher green path through a derelict farmstead and downhill to a stile and a plank bridge over a stream. Cross a field, heading for a stile in a hedge gap that leads onto the busy **Mersea Road**. Walk to the right down this road, with care. In 170 yards, past a house on your left, look for a footpath sign which points into **Man Wood** and walk fairly steeply down through this wood to a stile at the edge. Follow local waymarks to the banks of the **Roman River** and turn left for 70 yards to a bridge. Turn right over the bridge and cross the river. Walk up the slope to the left of a hedge and cross another stile onto a metalled track. Turn left and follow this track for 600 yards to the gates of an army depot. (2¹/₂ miles)

⑤ Bear right with the track and on reaching a wood turn right (northwards) along **Cherry Tree**

**Lane**. Follow this gravel lane for 800 yards. Look for and cross to your left at a metal gate by a roundabout of tracks. The wide grass track goes under power lines. Ignore crossing paths. Now the track goes down to cross a stream and up the other side. Walk uphill on this concrete track under some tall Scots pine trees. Turn left to negotiate a pond. Bear right (with arrows) through trees. At the end of the wood, turn right along a gravel track back to the car park. (1¹/₂ miles)

*Date walk completed:*

# TILLINGHAM TO SOUTHMINSTER

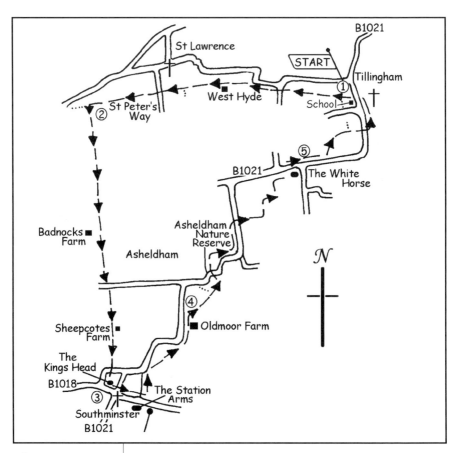

**Distance:**
8¹/₂ miles

**Starting point:**
West Park car park,
opposite the church
in Tillingham.
GR 993038

**Map: OS Explorer 176 Blackwater Estuary**

**How to get there:** *Tillingham is on the B1021 north of
Burnham-on-Crouch. Approaching from the west, turn off the
B1018 at Latchingdon and follow the signs to Bradwell
before going south to Tillingham. Opposite the church turn
westwards to West Park.*

ASHELDHAM NATURE RESERVE IS A TRANQUIL SPOT

*A* walk through the heart of the Dengie peninsula is an uplifting experience. This circuit begins by heading west from Tillingham, and reveals a beautiful aspect of the Blackwater Estuary and the boats that sail in it. It then turns south over slowly rolling hills and by ancient farm steadings to visit the village of Southminster, whose church, reputedly, contains furniture from Nelson's flagship, *Victory*. More glorious countryside follows on the way to Asheldham, home to the writer Samuel Bensusan. After passing through a nature reserve, the route crosses open fields to reach Dengie, before heading back to Tillingham for a welcome rest.

The **Kings Head** sits in a commanding position, at the crossroads in Southminster. Built as a three-roomed pub, like many others the building has been altered to offer a spacious interior. Outside you will find a beer garden and a large patio area, ideal for sunny days. There is a good selection of cooked meals and bar snacks on offer, with two or three beers from which to choose.

**Telephone:** *01621 772216.*

 *The Walk*

*Tillingham sits well inland behind its flats. Ducks used to be caught in the marshes hereabouts to provide the tables of rich London folk with a tasty morsel. The village street contains several ancient-looking weatherboarded dwellings, some of which, in fact, were only built around 1880. Tillingham's cottages are delightful, especially the long white-timbered one by the churchyard gate. Many of them were built by the Dean and Chapter of St Paul's, who for many hundreds of years have owned the land on which they stand.*

① From the car park walk alongside the cricket field, heading west. At the end of the field continue straight on into an arable field, with the hedge on your right. When the field ends, turn right over an earth bridge and immediately left. Bear right and

cross a bridge over the **Tillingham Brook**, soon reaching a road through two footpath posts. Here turn right and then left along the road to walk 300 yards to the next public footpath sign. Continue into the field and walk with the hedge on the left to **West Hyde**, a lone property. Here two waymarks set you on the right path. Aim for a hedge gap at the end of the next field. At another waymark cross a plank bridge and walk with the hedge on your right. At the hedge corner cross the next field, bearing left towards footpath posts at the end of the field. At this point cross the lane and follow the footpath post on a field edge, with a hedge and ditch on your right. In 250 yards, where the ditch turns left, a yellow arrow points right down into the next field. Cross the middle of this field, aiming for the right-hand edge of the wood ahead to a waymark and pass the wood to go over a plank bridge onto a crossing track. Turn right and immediately left over another plank bridge, now crossing a plantation of young trees to a yellow arrow waymark. All this time you have been walking part of the **St Peter's Way**, a 45 mile route from Ongar to Bradwell but in the opposite direction. (2 miles)

② Now turn left uphill on a broad green path heading south. Coming to a track, do not turn right with it but carry straight on, keeping trees and a hedge to your right. After barely ¹/₂ mile from the track, near a pylon, come to the **Asheldham Brook** and cross this by an earth bridge. Walk uphill with a hedge and ditch on your left. Halfway up cross left over another earth bridge

and continue with the hedge on your right to a point adjacent with **Badnocks Farm** on your right. Walk over the open field towards a cottage surrounded by fir trees. Close to the cottage is a gap in the firs. Go through this gap and turn left down the farm lane to the road. Briefly turn left and then right off the road up a bridleway to **Sheepcotes Farm**. Follow the track to the right of the farm buildings to arrive in front of a magnificent farmhouse, facing south. This can look spectacular, especially on a sunny day. Walk downhill, passing a large pond, to join **Sheepcotes**

THE KINGS HEAD, SOUTHMINSTER

Lane. This leads to **North End Road** at **Southminster**. Walk straight over into **Pump Mead Close**. A path to the left leads into **North Street**. Turn right past the **White Horse** pub to the **Kings Head** for your mid-walk break. (2½ miles)

*Dr Scott, the vicar of Southminster church from 1809 to 1840, was a great friend of Nelson. Indeed, he was the man in whose arms Nelson died on board the Victory. From that famous ship Scott brought Nelson's chart table, bureau and mirror and installed them in the vestry of Southminster church.*

③ After your stop at the pub, walk down **Station Road**. Just before reaching the **Station Arms** public house turn left into a twitten signed 'No cycling' at the entrance. Follow the twitten, crossing an estate road on the way to reach the main road. Turn right to the corner and again turn right into a field at a concrete public footpath sign. Do not follow the track which leads to the hall but cross the field diagonally to the left (north-east) to a gap in the hedge. Through the hedge the pathway becomes more clearly defined and this path leads to a concrete public footpath post. Turn right, following the road past **Oldmoor Farm**. (1 mile)

④ On reaching a footpath post, turn

right over a stile and walk with a fence on your right. Cross another stile. When the hedge finishes, continue on the same line across the field to a fence corner to follow the fence on your left and cross a stile and a bridge over the **Asheldham Brook**.

*In Asheldham you will experience countryside of the most tranquil nature. Where the land rises above the marshes, one can make out the features of a plateau camp used by the ancient Britons. Here were the bulwarks of our shores in ancient days. One of the two sets of earthworks encloses the church of St Lawrence which has a strong tower some 600 years old that has been restored in brick. One of the more famous immigrants of Essex was Samuel Bensusan, who left London in the early 20th century at the age of 36 to live in Asheldham. As a former London journalist, he was advised by his doctor to try the bracing air of the Essex coast to recover from illness. He set himself to apply his wonderfully descriptive and evocative style to do for the Essex marshes what Hardy did for Dorset. In his lifetime Bensusan wrote 60 books portraying the life and times of these parts.*

Ignore an arrow on your left and come to two step stiles. Take the right-hand one and cross the field to the right, heading for a tall metal gate. Go through this and cross a minor road. Follow the path to the left, passing the backs of two houses. In the garden of one there is a large pillbox from the Second World War. Soon you come to the main road at a stile. Cross this road with care to a footpath sign opposite. This leads into the **Asheldham Nature Reserve**. Turn right and follow the path parallel with the road. Turn left and join a footpath at the end of the reserve coming from the left. Turn right and cross the road with this path, following a fence on your right. Come to a yellow arrow and turn left with it at right angles to cross the field to trees and another yellow arrow pointing right. Follow that path with the edge of the field left and right to a bridge in the corner. Cross the bridge and walk straight over the next field leftish to the far corner. Turn left up a farm track and follow the arrow bearing right to a concrete public footpath sign at the road. Turn right and walk along the road as far as the **White Horse** pub at **Dengie**. (2 miles)

*Dengie gives its name to the whole area (the former 'hundred') and yet appears quite insignificant upon the map. Located east of Asheldham and south of Tillingham, it consists of a lane which goes nowhere in particular. The only access to the sea wall eastwards is the drive to The Grange and a subsequent footpath.*

⑤ Opposite the pub, cross the road and join a path at a footpath sign. Follow this well-marked path, taking the option to the right leading to the back of houses in **Tillingham**. Turn left and at a wide gap turn into **Chapel Road**, leading to the main street. Turn left along this, past the shops and pubs, back to the car park. (1 mile)

*Date walk completed:*

# LANGHAM TO DEDHAM HEATH

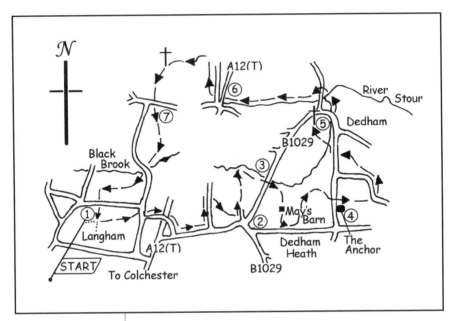

**Distance:**
11¼ miles

**Starting point:**
The Langham
Community Centre
car park.
GR 023318

**Map: OS Explorer 196 Sudbury, Hadleigh & Dedham Vale**

**How to get there:** *Langham lies to the west of the A12,
just north of Colchester. Follow the signs into Langham
from the A12. Head west along Park Lane to the T-junction,
then north to the Shepherd and Dog public house. Turn
right and very shortly you will come to the Langham
Community Centre on your right.*

SOUTH HILLS COTTAGE WITH ITS COLOURFUL GARDEN

*W*e think of this interesting circuit as the 'alternative Dedham walk' because it is part of, but quite different from, most of the routes we have previously walked around the village. Once over the busy A12, there is a lovely section round Hill House, Lamb Corner and Monk's Lane. It has everything – a delightful country location, a forest of chocolate box thatched cottages and an undulating lane. This is followed by a stroll along a river bank. More hills, May's Lane, and a short section of the Essex Way bring you to your 'out of town' lunch stop. Well rested you can resume your journey through historic Dedham, leaving just as much time as you choose to visit the sights. A tranquil river walk along the Stour brings you to the outskirts of Stratford St Mary and the long climb up to remote Langham church. Now comes perhaps our favourite bit of the walk over Black Brook and back to the car.

The **Anchor** at Dedham Heath makes an ideal stop for lunch. Food is served every day and includes a restaurant menu and bar snacks, together with a traditional roast on Sunday. Adnams, Greene King IPA, Stella, Carlsberg, Murphy's and Strongbow cider are the drinks available and there is a side garden where you can sit on fine days. It can get busy here at lunchtimes so it is advisable to book ahead.

**Telephone:** *01206 323131.*

# The Walk

① From the car park walk out over the sports field, keeping the hedge on your left, to the field corner and a stile. Turn left and head straight across the open field to walk just to the right of a small workshop area. You can see the words 'Powerplus Engineering' clearly across the field. Continue ahead to the stile. Cross the farm drive and another field to yet another stile. A short twitten brings you out to the road. Almost directly opposite take a similar footpath out to a stile and the road. Now follows nearly a mile of road walking. Turn left and go over the **A12** to a T-junction. Turn left again into **Birchwood Road**. Turn left a third time into **Boxhouse Lane**. You have now sampled three sides of the square made when the path directly over the **A12** was surrendered to traffic. When you are level with **Newfoundland Lodge**, turn right almost through the hedge at the brown footpath direction post. Cross the stile and a lovely open meadow to a further stile. Make your way out onto a concrete track leading to the road and the very pretty houses at **Lamb Corner**. (2 miles)

② Turn left into **Monk's Lane** which starts off as a quiet road, becomes a grass track and then a footpath, as for over ³/₄ mile, it dips, climbs, turns left and right and, finally, descends to a stream which we think is a continuation of **Black Brook**. At this point, turn right and walk with the brook on your left to eventually go through a garden and out to the **B1029**. (1 mile)

③ Turn left and walk down the road to **Freemans Farm** (if the diversion notices are still around, worry not – FP 43 is unaffected). Turn right and cross the farmyard to a small green gate and walk uphill with the hedge on your left. At the first yellow arrow keep straight on. At the next arrow go left through a kissing gate and right up **May's Barn** drive. At the road turn left. In about ¹/₄ mile turn left again up a double-hedged track next to **Alumhurst**. At the first open field head half right to the next hedgerow. Now get on to circular walk 2, heading north. There are good views of **Dedham church** from here. When the hedge ends go half right across the field to a yellow arrow and bridge. Walk along this remote lane, passing eye-catching **South Hills Cottage**. After a few more yards look for another sign for circular walk 2 and turn right up the gravel drive to and then left in front of **The Orchard**. Just past the house and garden turn right up a very narrow uphill path, cross a stile,

cross the next field to a stile and turn right at the road. Walk past **Anchor Lane** till you come to the pub and your lunch. (1³/₄ miles)

④ Suitably refreshed, retrace your steps to **Anchor Lane** and turn right, following the footpath across five stiles to the road. Turn left and walk downhill to the sharp left corner. Take the footpath going half left across the field and climb the stile. Your route continues north-west across a field and track and another field to a footpath sign. Go down the narrow fenced path just to the right of the school. When you come out on the road turn right and walk

THE ANCHOR, DEDHAM HEATH

for about 1/8 mile to turn left into **Southfields**. Follow the footpath into the playing fields (a good spot for a picnic). You are just at the rear of **Dedham church**. Walking on past the toilets into **Dedham High Street** you will find yourself right behind the war memorial. (1 3/4 miles)

*Dedham was important as a centre for the wool industry during the 13th and 14th centuries. It has a magnificent church built about 1500 by Thomas Webbe, a merchant who lies buried in the north aisle. Facing the church in the High Street you will find a fantastic collection of old buildings, an inn, a tearoom, the war memorial and an art and craft centre. There are also numerous reminders of the town's famous painters, Constable and Munnings. As Flatford Mill is only about a mile away, the village centre can get very busy on fine summer days. It is on the regular coach tour route for Constable Country which is why we have chosen to eat well away from the centre and just walk through the village on our way back to Langham.*

⑤ Turn right and walk past **Dedham Art and Craft Centre**. As the road bends right, take the path on your left, which starts up the drive to **Fountain House** and **Down**

**Hall**. Turn left through a kissing gate and walk to the right of the pond. Pass a yellow arrow and go through the next kissing gate to continue past the rear of the car park. Stay on this narrow path to the concrete road and the river. Turn left and walk out to the road and **Dedham Mill**. Turn right and then, immediately after the mill, left along the footpath and over the weir and bridge. Pass **Dedham Lock** on your left, then descend the steps to go through the kissing gate and turn left to walk along the left-hand side of the field. You will soon find yourself strolling along the banks of the **River Stour**, another lovely place for a picnic. After a series of kissing gates, you come to the very edge of the **A12**. Go through the final gate and then through the tunnel under this busy road. (1 1/2 miles)

⑥ Turn right and walk north up the road for 1/2 mile towards **Stratford St Mary**. When you come to **Weir Cottage**, turn left over the weir and a stile. You now continue over the open field towards a gate. Cross the stile beside the gate and turn left up a hedged path until you come to a 'Private' sign. Turn right and cross the horse track and walk ahead with the hedge on your right. You will quickly come to a gravel crossing track with a sign for the **Essex Way** and a yellow arrow. Turn left and (you have guessed it) up the track to **Langham church**. Walk past the church and down the wide private drive and out onto the road by the footpath sign. (1$^1/_2$ miles)

*Langham is famous for its 13th-century church tower which John Constable climbed in order to paint views of the Stour valley. He was friendly with John Fisher, the rector, who offered to make him schoolmaster in the village. It was John Fisher's nephew, another John Fisher, who became one of Constable's life-long friends.*

⑦ Take the path opposite, up the farm drive that serves **Glebe House**, **Sunnyside Farm** and **Glebe Farm**. When the drive splits, keep right uphill, passing a white painted house on your right. Follow the direction indicated by the blue arrow down a very narrow path to walk past the beautiful pink and timber **Priory Cottage** to the road. Turn left to a footpath sign on your right. Cross the stile and the adventure begins over **Black Brook**. This very low lying area can get somewhat wet at times. Cross a stile, and then a stile and bridge with plenty of yellow arrows over the deeper stream bed. Now head half left uphill to a stile with more yellow arrows. This narrow fenced path crosses a further stile and goes under the sweet smelling eucalyptus trees with a wire fence on your right. You will walk through what looks to be someone's back garden. However, you will find several familiar yellow arrows through here, which confirm you have not in fact gone wrong. Cross a stile, walk through the bracken on a narrow path, and pass through a small wood to a gate. You will now enter a large field. Walk to the right of the pond to the far corner and another gate. The wide green lane narrows as you pass hen houses on your right. Cross a stile and start looking for a path off left with no waymarks. The path leads you directly to a clearly visible kissing gate. Go through this and walk with the hedge on your left, then between two houses out to the road. You will find **Langham Community Centre** straight ahead where your transport awaits. (1$^3/_4$ miles)

*Date walk completed:*

# GREAT OAKLEY TO TENDRING

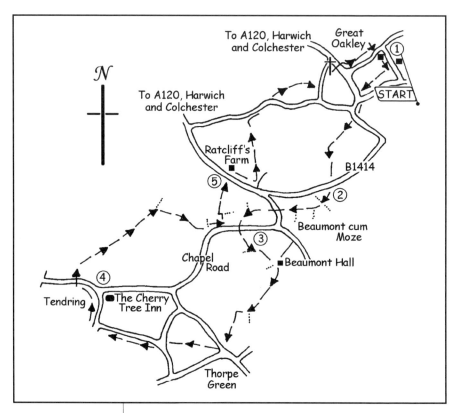

**Distance:**
10¹/₂ miles

**Starting point:**
By the war
memorial in
Great Oakley.
GR 196275

Map: OS Explorer 184 Colchester

**How to get there:** *Great Oakley is located off the A120 Colchester to Harwich road. From the west, pass Horsley Cross and leave the main road on the right, signposted to Wix. Continue through Wix village and after 1¹/₂ miles you will reach Great Oakley where you should turn left along the village street. Turn right just past the war memorial and park nearby.*

'*A* round the Moze' has a certain ring to it and this area south-west of Harwich is rightly admired, though little known in greater Essex. We are talking here of Great Oakley, Beaumont cum Moze, Thorpe Green and Tendring. Great Oakley is a wonderful old village and some of its houses date back 400 years. Beaumont cum Moze spreads over several streets and has some very attractive houses as well as a fine hall and church. Thorpe Green on the fringe of Thorpe le Soken is bounded by a magnificent private property known as Bradley Hall. Tendring is a Saxon village with a 17th-century hall containing old ceiling beams. We connect all these places in a most attractive walk. It is fairly flat, though the route from Beaumont Hall drops several feet towards Thorpe le Soken. There are fine views to the east over the Naze to the North Sea.

The **Cherry Tree Inn** is on the corner of Crow Lane and the B1035 east of Tendring village. This is a fine pub by any standards. Just look at the real ales: Adnams Bitter and Regatta, Greene King IPA and Abbot. There is also Strongbow on draught for cider lovers. Snack eaters have a good choice of jacket potatoes, sandwiches and ploughman's and, if a more substantial meal is desired there is a large choice of main courses on a blackboard. On a regular à la carte menu, a further selection of most attractive main courses and desserts will take your eye.

**Telephone:** *01255 830340.*

 *The Walk*

① From **Great Oakley village** pass by the **Maybush** public house and at the back of the houses turn right off the lane and follow a path south-west to join the **B1414** road. Turn left past **Workhouse Corner** and **Cabbage Row**. Join a footpath to your right leading south-west across the fields. You join and follow a ditch and later cross right by a plank bridge. Turn left (your original direction) and soon come to the site of **Buck's Farm**. Bear left along a narrow concrete track for 150 yards and reach a road. (1¹/₂ miles)

② Cross the road and follow the path to the right. When you come

GREAT OAKLEY TO TENDRING

**GREAT OAKLEY VILLAGE STREET**

to a small wood turn right for 15 yards and turn left over a bridge through the wood. Later, pass by a large reservoir. Cross a road and follow the path, bearing left over a plank bridge to a wood on your right. Look for a stile buried in the wood and cross this onto a path leading south to the side of a house. Pass to the left of a shed and over another stile out to **Chapel Road** in **Beaumont cum Moze**. Turn right along **Chapel Road** and after 50 yards join a farm track on the left at a footpath sign. (1 mile)

③ Walk on the track, soon turning right. Spot a waymark sign on the left at an oak tree and cross into the field above, walking round the field edge to the left and uphill to another waymark. Now turn right and walk towards a fenceway at the boundary of **Beaumont Hall**, a private residence.

*Here there is a fine group of buildings of long ago – the red-*

*tiled barns, the timbered house with charming Dutch gables, and the little church. The chancel walls, a doorway, and a buttress or two, are 600 years old; the altar and the altar rails are 18th century. From the hill on which this small church stands there is a splendid view seaward of the salt marshes, worked in Norman times, and we may think that since those days no braver man than Lord Byng, 1st Viscount Byng of Vimy, has lived here. He died in 1935 and it was he who led the Canadians to victory at Vimy Ridge near Arras in the First World War. There is a local story that he happened on a sergeant abusing a horse. Not in uniform, he spoke to the sergeant, who replied, 'You get it down the road yourself.' Byng calmed the horse and duly led it down to the end of the road.*

Continue on this good path, and when you reach the hall turn right to another fenceway and walk south downhill with fine views. About 100 yards before the hedge ahead, turn right at a waymark over a bridge and cross a field on a cross-field path (usually marked) to an oak tree with a yellow arrow. Cross a ditch to the left and turn right for a few yards, then left again through a thicket and out to a road. Cross the road and follow the cut path at **Thorpe Green** to a footpath sign.

126

*Thorpe le Soken, just south-east of Thorpe Green, is one of the three Sokens in Essex (Thorpe, Kirby and Walton). In Saxon times, a soke meant a place which enjoyed certain privileges. The settlements are extremely ancient and were granted to the canons of St Paul's, London by King Athelstan, who died 126 years before the arrival of William the Conqueror.*

Walk behind houses and over a field to cross an airstrip. Join a path with a hedge on your left to a lane south of **Bradley Hall**. A short path across a field links two concrete footpath posts; then you turn right and walk along a narrow lane. You pass **Hill House** and cross a stream to reach the road. Turn right and go past the **Manor House**, continuing to the **Cherry Tree Inn** for your lunch break. (3 miles)

④ Leave the pub and walk towards **Tendring village**. In the village, spot a footpath sign and turn right along a wide track. At the fence corner on your right, which coincides with the end of the wood on your left, a long straight path runs half right for 3/4 mile to the angle of woods marking the boundary of the

THE CHERRY TREE INN, TENDRING

fields. At the woods cross three bridges in succession and turn left along the wood running north-east. At the end of this wood turn sharp right and walk south-east up the field to the right-hand corner where you will identify two waymarks at a slightly difficult ditch crossing onto a grassy track leading to **Lucas's Farm**. Keep on, past a footpath sign, to the road at **Beaumont**. Turn left round a corner by some beautiful houses and turn left at a second footpath sign into a field. After 20 yards, turn right and walk to the field edge. Here turn left and follow the edge for 3/4 mile to **Ratcliff's Farm**. (2¹/₂ miles)

⑤ At the road turn right and walk to the area known as **the Oak**. Turn left at a footpath sign and follow a concrete track. When it bears right, leave the track and continue north by a field path to join another concrete path at the left end of a hedge. This continues to a minor road. Turn right along this road for about 500 yards to the point where the road turns sharp right. Turn left off the road here and follow a footpath post right along a field edge. Soon you pass a large

reservoir and continue along the next field by the edge. Pass through a gap in the hedge and 200 yards later turn right into a farmstead and immediately turn left. When the path turns right, carry straight on along an overgrown path and over a stile out to the road. Turn left and pass **Great Oakley church** to turn right up a footpath beside it. When you soon reach a road turn right and then left into **Great Oakley village street**. Presently you reach the war memorial and your car. (2¹/₂ miles)

*Sycamores guard Great Oakley churchyard and oaks and chestnuts grow in profusion. A Norman window tells us how long a church has been here, and the square font with 20 round-headed panels has been in use all through the church's history. Up in the chancel is a doorway of 1500, now closed forever, enriched with carvings of angels, crowns and heads. The east window is filled with portraits of saints and angels, and strikes a delightful colour note seen through the pointed chancel arch.*

*Date walk completed:*